The
A to Z
of Love, Sex and Exasperation

The A to Z
of Love, Sex and Exasperation

Everything You Need to Know to Survive and be Happy

DENISE ROBERTSON

Illustrations by Brian Gibson

To all those people who have written to me over the years about their relationships. I'm grateful to them for all they've taught me about human relationships and I hope they have all found the fulfilment they deserve.

First published in the United Kingdom in 2012
by Max Press, Little Books Ltd,
73 Campden Hill Towers, 112 Notting Hill Gate, London W11 3QP.

10 9 8 7 6 5 4 3 2 1

Text © by Denise Robertson
Design and layout © by Max Press
Illustrations © by Brian Gibson

All rights reserved. No part of this work may be reproduced or utilised in any form or by any means, electronic or mechanical, including photocopying, recording or by any information storage and retrieval system, without the prior written permission of the publisher.

ISBN: 978 1 906264 21 5

The author and publisher will be grateful for any information that will assist them in keeping future editions up-to-date. Although all reasonable care has been taken in the preparation of this book, neither the publisher, editors nor the author can accept any liability for any consequences arising from the use thereof, or the information contained therein.

Printed and bound by CPI Group (UK) Ltd, Croydon, CR0 4YY

There is nothing quite as supportive and exhilarating as a good relationship. Alas, you have to kiss a few frogs along the way before you find your prince or princess. I hope this book will help you endure that journey and, when you find your dream lover, make the very most of it.

HE SAYS: The direct question, 'Do you want to sleep with me?' is mindless. Unless all your testosterone suddenly drained through your big toe, of course you want to sleep with her, but say 'Yes' (the honest answer) at your peril. You will be told that all men are the same and after one thing. Lie through your teeth and say 'No', and the heavens will open. 'What's wrong with me? Why don't you fancy me? You should have told me I wasn't your type,' – and on and on.

> *SHE SAYS: For men, sex is like oxygen. They can't take it or leave it.*

HE SAYS: 'Was that all right for you?' is not a polite question; it's a cry from the heart. Say, 'I suppose so,' or 'Uh-huh,' and you condemn us to lie awake, staring down the dark, trying to choose between penis enhancement or Viagra.

> *SHE SAYS: Men, especially your colleagues, seldom look anywhere else but your boobs. Sometimes you think your voice must be coming from your left nipple, so rapt is their attention.*

HE SAYS: Today, with women putting everything in the shop window, a man's groin is activated hourly – which is why we haven't discovered anything much since the bagless vacuum cleaner.

Affairs

Some affairs creep up on you, often at work. Others are entered into deliberately: in the hope of livening up a relationship, to get back at your partner, or simply because of lust. We now live in a comparatively liberal society, but affairs are still generally frowned upon. The National Centre for Social Research has been surveying social attitudes since 1983. In that year, 85 per cent of those interviewed said they thought infidelity was wrong. This year the figure was 86 per cent, with 91 per cent of women saying it is wrong to be sexually unfaithful. Compare those figures, not only unchanged but slightly increased, with the figure for disapproval of sex before marriage. In 1983, 28 per cent thought it wrong. Now only seven per cent do. Perhaps the high level of disapproval springs from the knowledge that affairs spell trouble, even though, in another study, a report

A

into marriage breakdown, it would seem that people are less likely to end a relationship because of infidelity than once obtained.

If you're found out in an affair, trust has gone from your relationship and it's hard to get it back. If you're the one who discovers your partner's affair, you will feel betrayed, and probably – and crazily – guilty. Where did you go wrong? How did you fail them? What did the other man/woman have that you lack? The answer is you didn't fail; you weren't found lacking; and all the other person had over you was the smack of danger. Relationships are safe, and safe can mean boring. You see one another 24/7, and you may each cease to make the effort to attract. In an affair, both sides try harder. There's no cocoa and carpet slippers watching *Corrie*. It's all secret meetings and using dental floss to keep your breath sweet. But if that affair turned into a relationship and you didn't keep up the effort, it could get boring too.

If you're hankering after an affair, or even in the middle of one, ask yourself why you're doing it. Have you met the love of your life, in which case just own up to your partner? Or do you simply like having a bit on the side? Are you trying to live out a fantasy, or was drink to blame? Is the affair simply an escape from a relationship that's stressful, or that has run out of steam? Or is the affair comforting, in that it helps you not to think about the C word – commitment?

A

If you're the one who has strayed, answer these questions:

♥ Was it just sexual?

♥ Is it a one-off, or one of many?

♥ Are you ready to relinquish your relationship if the affair comes to light?

♥ Have you really tried to keep your relationship alive, or did you take your partner for granted?

You need to answer those questions before you begin to think of solutions or talking it through with an independent third party. See the Help section at the end. And perhaps try to rebuild your life.

If you're the injured party these questions are for you:

♥ Has your partner showed remorse?

♥ Was your sexual relationship good before the affair?

♥ Is what you would lose if you split more important than hurt pride?

A

If your answer to that last question is Yes, you need to talk things through with someone who can help you sort out your tangled emotions and begin to rebuild. See the Help section at the end.

One word of warning: tit-for-tat affairs end in tears.

Age difference

Convention dictates that, unless a man and a woman are in the same age group, the man should be older than the woman. Today's woman knows this is nonsense, and the term 'toy-boy' has been coined for a younger man in a relationship with an older woman. Relate claims more couples than ever are marrying despite an age gap, and the average gap has grown, from two years in 2000 to eight in 2011. For many couples the gap is much greater, but what is the truth about age differences? Can May mate with December? Is a man or woman foolish to embark on a relationship with a much younger partner?

There is no golden rule. Relationships with a difference of 20 years or more have endured and flourished. But there are a couple of things to consider. Do either of the partners want children; and does the age discrepancy interfere with conception? Men's fertility extends well into old age, though it diminishes slowly after 50. Women are capable of child-bearing

A

up until the menopause, which, for most women, occurs around the age of 50, but fertility is waning before that point.

Other than that, my only worry would be when one partner or the other is immature. The boy or girl of 17 may bear little resemblance to the man or woman they become at 40. Until roughly the age of 25, we change physically, mentally, and emotionally. The person who is your soul mate at 17 may have nothing in common with you at 30. So worry less about the age difference, and more about the emotional maturity of your partner. If they are still in their teens or early 20s, take the relationship slowly and see how things develop. Although age difference can be overcome, it should always be carefully thought through.

Aphrodisiacs

If you're daft enough to believe that an oyster can improve or impair desire, this book is not for you.

Appearance

There's no doubt that appearance plays a part in attraction. A study by Columbia University found that single people

A

hoping to get married rate potential partners on both their physical and socio-economic attraction, but that other factors, such as sense of humour and intelligence, also play a part. Another recent survey found that four out of five women surveyed lacked confidence. Just 15 per cent felt sufficiently self-assured to initiate love-making with their partner. Even fewer had the courage to go skinny-dipping. Although men are more reticent about admitting to any lack of confidence, their letters to me over the years suggest they are no more sure of themselves – just better at putting on a front.

You should care about looking your best, making the most of good points and trying to minimise the bad ones. Frequently, worries about appearance centre around weight. According to a survey by diet experts, the women surveyed said food and its effect on them meant more to them than sex, and that they put more effort into dieting than into their relationships. One in four women dieters in the survey confessed that dieting was more important to them than a relationship; and 54 per cent thought more about food than sex, and regarded cheating on a diet as worse than betraying a lover. Three-quarters of women in Britain – more than 22 million – have been on a diet at least once in their lifetime. The perfect body is still the aim, but one in women in seven says it was cruel comments about their weight that drove them to diet.

These are pretty depressing findings. If you feel any of them could apply to you, you need to think seriously about whether or not your priorities are right, and your level of self-esteem as high as it should be. Finding your right weight isn't easy, but it's worth it for your health's sake. Trouble comes when that desire to be slim goes too far, and tips into an eating disorder. If that happens to you, seek help immediately (see Help section), because disorders like anorexia and bulimia can ruin your appearance.

In recent times, the demand for cosmetic surgery (about 10 per cent) and non-surgical intervention (90 per cent) has soared. The latest survey estimates that it grew by 17 per cent between 2008 and 2010, and the industry is now thought to be worth £2.3 billion a year. Face lifts, gastric bypasses, tummy tucks, liposuction, and breast augmentation or reduction are becoming more common, where once they were rare. Last year, doctors carried out 9,430 breast enlargements, 3,417 tummy tucks, nearly 5,000 facelifts, more than 4,000 nose jobs, and more than 1,000 operations to correct ears that stuck out. These were all surgical interventions making up the 10 per cent. We can only guess at the number of Botox injections and the like which made up the 90 per cent. Surgery to correct disfigurement can be hugely beneficial, but what level of asymmetry or abnormality is required to justify breast surgery? When do

A

large breasts create enough of a physical problem to need treatment? When is a size B bra cup a handicap? Most women (and I suspect more men than confess it) are dissatisfied with their appearance to some extent, often without cause. Sometimes this can be so severe that it becomes body dysmorphic disorder, and requires expert help. Usually it's based on low self-esteem, and may have no real foundation whatsoever. If friends and family you trust tell you your nose or your boobs are fine, believe them and be proud of your body. If there's real room for improvement check out the experts carefully before you choose one.

Clothes: There's no doubt that the right dress, the right suit, can send a man or woman striding confidently into the mating market place. But if the need to dress up becomes an addiction, you should do some thinking. The right clothes don't guarantee the right relationship. If a man or woman values you on the clothes you wear, do you want their approval? Acquire a wardrobe of clothes you are comfortable with, clothes in which you feel good; make sure they're well cared for; and then accept them for the accessories they are.

There are a few tricks that can help. If you're buying off the peg, it's worth finding a good dressmaker who can tweak the new garment to your exact size, or add that little extra something which makes your dress that bit different. That

A

gives you that made-to-measure feel. And if you have a dress or a suit you adore, which is now too shabby to wear, a good dressmaker or tailor can copy it. Cut out pictures of garments you really admire, and show them to assistants in busy stores. They may know where something similar is lurking. But don't feel you have to 'buy new' for every special occasion. If the royal family can recycle, so can we. And don't forget grooming. You can't be well-turned out with laddered tights, or a gravy stain on your tie.

Make-up: Once upon a time cosmetics and toiletries were a female province. No longer. Men can moisturise and spray with the best of them, and the British make-up market has hit the £1 billion mark largely because of the advent of metrosexual man, and the fact that glamour is in vogue. There is no doubt that cosmetics properly applied are a huge confidence booster, so don't be afraid to seek advice. But if cosmetics become a mask behind which you hide, if the thought of waking up next to a man with your face bare sends you scurrying for a hiding place, you are becoming too dependent on them and losing faith in your own natural good looks. One survey found that some women even spray hair lacquer over their make-up to set it and sleep in bedsocks filled with moisturiser to avoid wrinkled feet. If you're tempted to go that far, pause and consider (see Self-esteem).

A

Arguments

In a healthy relationship, argument is understandable. If these arguments are few and far between and end in a mutual backing-down, then you're lucky.

A 'good' argument, one that is conducted fairly, is much better than putting up with something unfair and simmering with resentment or, worst of all, sulking. And the very fact that you live together, or spend most of your leisure time in one another's company, means that you will come in for a major part of the disgruntlement in your partner that we all feel at times. So the fact that the two of you argue is not, in itself, a sign that you'd be better apart. However, if the arguments are almost constant and spring up for no good reason, you need to ask some questions:

♥ Are you becoming the victim of your partner's bad moods, their verbal punch-bag, simply because they're unhappy with their lot and, unlike acquaintances, you can't just walk away?
♥ Did the arguing start after an incident or has it crept into the relationship?
♥ Is the reason for the argument valid, or simply an excuse for something they resent, for instance that you don't praise them, especially over their sexual expertise?

A

- Is your partner taking pleasure in putting you down because it makes them feel big?
- Do they always have to win, even when they're patently in the wrong?
- Have arguments become a habit, something to enliven an otherwise dull day?

If you're the one doing the arguing, can you answer these questions:

- Do you start arguments for trivial reasons because, deep down, you feel you're not getting a fair deal from your partner?
- Do you take out the irritations of your working day on your partner?
- Does having a row give you a buzz?
- Do you get a kick out of winning?
- Are you bored in the relationship, and ready to do anything to relieve it?
- Has something in the past made you someone who expects to be slighted, and reacts to offence where none is intended?
- Did you argue in previous relationships?

A

Whether you're the one who starts arguments or the one who feels on the end of them, if you answered yes to any of the questions in either quiz, you need a frank discussion with your partner. If that fails, if you need help to sort out what is going on, Relate will help you work out whether the arguments you have are energising your relationship or eating it away. Sometimes the things your partner says may hide their true feelings. 'Why are you so demanding?' may really mean, 'You only want me for sex.' 'Why don't you want it any more?' is not about sex alone, it's asking 'Am I loved?'

A common cause of argument is responsibility, who should see to what. Are you taking your fair share of responsibility for contraception, household chores, financial security? And are rows down to some other factor such as stress, tiredness, alcohol, hormones, or cramped conditions in the home? If you can pin down the cause, you're half-way to abolishing rows for ever.

When it comes to the discussion, pick your time. Research shows that people tend to be more amenable early in the day, but increasingly negative as the day wears on. So, if you time your discussion for that moment after a hard day at the office, when you're beginning to think wistfully of bed, you're not going to get far. Choose a weekend or a day off, and try to create a happy atmosphere. Talking when things are

A

going right is 100 per cent more effective. Don't labour your points, make them, and then listen respectfully while your partner counters them. Try to deal with one thing at a time, and not heap in all those other little niggles like the lavatory seat and towels on the bathroom floor. Don't feel you simply *have* to win. What you want is the right outcome, one that promises peace in the future. And if you and your partner can't resolve it together, see the Help section.

An occasional row can clear the air, and making up afterwards can be particularly pleasant. If you are rowing often and for little or no reason, however, you need to look at the underlying relationship. Is there resentment on either side? Are there stresses on the work front or within the wider family? If no such factors exist, and you are both simply volatile and ready to fight at the drop of a hat, it can help to have a truce object, some ludicrous ornament which, once produced, brings with it a 15-minute silence. At the end of that time, hopefully there'll be nothing you wish to fight about (*see also* Confrontation).

HE SAYS: *Next time I'm coming back as a woman. I mean, who wouldn't settle for multiple orgasms?*

> SHE SAYS: *The fact that women can do three things at once is a source of annoyance to men, but that doesn't stop them expecting her to massage their ego with one hand, sugar their tea with the other, and rock the cradle with her foot.*

HE SAYS: *Today's female in full cry is the best laxative known to man.*

> SHE SAYS: *Male spending on gym membership, grooming products, and cosmetic surgery has rocketed. Man has become his own love object — not so much in touch with his feminine side as engulfed by it.*

HE SAYS: *Women have the ultimate weapon: they refuse you sex, and you're putty. No one's died from lack of it, but lack of it makes you wish you were dead.*

> SHE SAYS: *Ask for reassurance and all you get is, 'I'm not the romantic type,' or even worse, 'You know I can't say things like that.' Well, yes he can. He has a tongue. He thinks. He can say, 'Will you iron my rugby shirt?' quick enough.*

B

Baggage

We are all influenced by our past. Painful childhoods, difficult adolescence, a broken relationship . . . they mark us through and through, like the rings of a tree trunk. Upbringing tends to set our emotional clock. If emotion was frowned on then, if conversation was restrained, if sex was a taboo subject, we are probably not going to wind up as raving extroverts. If, on the other hand, ours was a noisy, boisterous, let-it-all-hang-out upbringing, chances are we won't be into restraint.

This disparity can often lead to misunderstandings. One person's silence is seen as sulking; the other's ebullience is seen as lack of sensitivity. Unless you can come to understand your different backgrounds, you will constantly be at loggerheads. In fact, each of you could be the perfect foil for the other, so it's worth trying to get it right. The other legacy of the past is trauma. If you've been betrayed before, you may find it hard

B

to trust. Perhaps one of you has a child or children, a living reminder that you have loved before and been let down, or bereaved. If you find your partner's children scary, or you feel the past is intruding into your relationship, turn to the Help section (*see also* Children). What you mustn't do is try to airbrush your partner's past out of the picture. You may get their family, their children, out of their life. You will never get them out of their heart. Nor can he or she simply forget betrayal or bereavement. With help, they can relegate them to the past, where they belong.

Bereavement

In the immediate aftermath of the death of a partner, you have tasks to complete, questions to answer. You are kept busy. This does not lessen the pain of loss, but it does supply a framework for getting through the day. You have to get up each morning, make decisions, function – and probably supply comfort to others who mourn just as you do. When all the decisions are made, and the mourners melt away, you suddenly realise you are alone. There will be times when you will see no reason for living, when the pain of loss will threaten to engulf you. Quite probably you'll want to move house. Resist the impulse. It may make sense to move, but do it when things have settled down. Turn to people who will understand your sense of loss and help you begin the healing process. At first memories may be unbearable, photographs a trigger for tears. You'll be unable to dispose of anything that was part of that life together, and the idea of a new life will seem almost obscene. But when you have had a wonderful relationship, it doesn't need a sad, weeping figure as a memorial. The one thing a loving partner wants is for the one they love to be happy; and death doesn't change that. Nor does a subsequent new love obliterate the love that was and still is. Does a second child delete the love you felt for your firstborn? So it is with a new relationship. New love grows, but it's wise to take time over forming new friendships. And remember there are people who understand the grieving process, and they're there for you if you need them (see Help section).

Betrayal

Can you ever forgive betrayal? The answer is 'sometimes'. Some people find it impossible, even though they may try very hard. Before forgiveness can take place, you need to take a long, hard look at what happened; and Marriage Care or Relate can be very helpful here (see Help section). Did your partner go out seeking sex with someone, or was it a

B

friendship that crept up on him or her, and turned sexual almost unintentionally? Were you in any way to blame in the run-up to the betrayal? Was your relationship under stress, or had you ceased to be engaged in it as much as before? Is your partner truly sorry, and does his or her contribution to your happiness alleviate the pain of what they did? These are the questions that must be answered before you can move on.

If you both work at it, a relationship can be stronger after coming through a crisis. This doesn't happen in every case – sometimes it's better to part. But if you have at least tried to reconcile and failed, you can say that you did your best (*see also* Infidelity and Serial Adultery).

TEN REASONS TO WALK AWAY

1. You start to dread meetings.
2. His or her temper flares frequently.
3. You feel relieved when home-time comes.
4. You suggest something, he/she says: 'If you like.'
5. They enthuse about someone they've just met – and then enthuse again.
6. They never talk of the future.
7. They tell you they're not the settling type.
8. They put you down.
9. They want you to change your appearance or beliefs.
10. They rubbish your friends or family.

B

Biological clock

The thought of your child-bearing years running out like sand from a broken egg-timer can be terrifying. You may not actually want a child, but the thought that you can no longer have one can be scary. Nor does it affect only women: psychologists believe that both sexes can have an instinctive reaction, usually around the age of 30, which makes them yearn for parenthood, and settle for an unsatisfactory relationship simply to make conception possible. To say this is a recipe for disaster is an understatement.

Fertility actually starts to decline in the 20s. After age 35, the rate of decline increases because women are born with a finite number of eggs and, in time, the supply runs out. If you're older, especially over 40, conceiving may not be easy, but that doesn't mean it's impossible. The number of women over the age of 30 having babies has risen in recent decades, and help for infertility has improved immensely. Two friends of mine conceived at 48, one a first baby and the other after a gap of 24 years. When you're over 35, some experts believe you have a higher chance of having a multiple pregnancy, whether or not there are twins in the family. Your chance of conceiving quickly, however, does depend on your age. Women are most fertile between the ages of 20 and 24. It can take longer to get pregnant when you hit your late 30s or

B

early 40s, but if you've been trying for a while it's wise to seek advice sooner rather than later. Make an appointment to see your GP after six months of trying to conceive (this means having sex two to three times a week).

Age also affects male fertility. As men age, their testosterone levels naturally decline and, in turn, their sex drive may wane. The quality of a man's semen also drops with age. Despite this fact, men continue to produce sperm for their entire lives and can procreate even into old age.

Body language

I'm uneasy about citing body language as a definite indication of intention, or lack of it, because some people are very good actors and can mimic being attentive or attracted; and others are naturally shy, which can inhibit their body movements. If you are talking to someone and their eye wanders, they may indeed be scouring the room for someone better to talk to – or they may be too shy to meet your eye. The person who fusses over you effusively may be unbelievably taken with you. He or she may also be one of those awful kissy-kissy people who haven't a true bone in their body. The man who stays as far away from you on the sofa as is humanly possible may be afraid of coming on too strong if he moves closer. The woman who doesn't give you a smile may simply be scared to death.

So the best advice I can give you is to trust your instinct. If you're attracted to someone and would like to know them better, use your own body language to ensure they know you are interested. If you're encouraged by their response, make sure they know how to contact you. If their body language makes you uncertain about whether your interest in them is welcome, don't be put off. Still make sure they know who and where you are, and then leave it to them.

Boredom

When you hear that a relationship is over the usual reasons spring to mind: infidelity, disagreement over money and goods, even abuse. Seldom, if ever, do we blame boredom, and yet a survey by a broadsheet newspaper found that women are more than eight times more likely to cite boredom with their partner as reason for divorce. A recent survey of family lawyers revealed that intolerance or growing apart is more often cited as the reason for divorce, and it is that 'growing apart' that is also responsible for the break-up of relationships that have not got as far as the altar. 'There's nothing left,' one partner or the other will say. The flame that drew them together has burned out. Sex has become infrequent, or ceased to sparkle ... there's no reason

B

to stay together. This is not anyone's fault. Neither party was lacking. The relationship that seemed so dynamic in the beginning simply ran out of steam.

Sometimes, with professional help, the spark can be re-ignited. More often it's best to chalk it down to experience and move on. Sadly, people find this hard. They either grow disproportionately angry and feel 'dumped', or they start to over-analyse their own behaviour, desperately searching for something they did wrong, some area where they were lacking. This is when the orgy of texting and emails can begin. Even worse, penitent calls begging for another chance. Instead of pestering your ex, spend time taking stock. Did the relationship really fizzle out, or was it that each of you had ceased to make an effort? A recent study showed that, on average, married couples gave up on romance two and a half years into marriage. If it can be so for others, is that what happened to you? Did you expect your partner to make all the effort? Did they cease to woo you? And, the 64,000-dollar question, if you did give up, are you both willing to try again to put the pzazz back into your relationship?

If, after careful consideration, you see that what you had may have been good but what is left is dead as a dodo, don't despair. Don't think you're jinxed and doomed to live alone. Don't reach for phone or keyboard. Be thankful that a poor relationship has now ended, making room for one that will.

B

Breaking up

The end of a relationship can feel like the end of the world. It's not. It can hurt like hell, but it's not fatal. Look around you: the world is full of people whose lives did not end when they split up. As Shakespeare said, 'Men have died from time to time, and worms have eaten them – but not for love.'

When you lose a partner it leaves a hole in your life and holes are painful. Sometimes the fear of that pain – of being alone – can keep you in a relationship that is no longer alive. You reason that something is better than nothing. You may think you need a partner to make you whole; after all, the rest of the world seems to be paired off. Better to be miserable in partnership than the odd one out. This is wrong thinking. If you're with the wrong person, with someone who puts you down, or betrays you, or simply fails to make your heart beat faster, you're better off alone. That way there's room for new things to develop.

Now, that's easy for me to say, but you may have invested time, energy, love, even money in this relationship, and you still hope for a return. Besides, you want someone to moan to at the end of a working day, someone who'll rub your back when it aches or give you a cuddle when you are down. All those things are precious, but they don't make up for that gnawing feeling in your gut that this relationship is dead. Of

B

course you'll cry when it's over; you'll pick up the phone to text him or her; you'll search Facebook to see if he or she has surfaced. You'll comfort-eat or drink too much, or pick a row with someone over nothing. But eventually life will cease to rock on its foundations, you'll feel a sense of relief – relief that lets you start to plan (see Survival).

If you feel you've been cruelly dumped, you have to accept what has occurred. You can't make your ex behave decently, but you do have control over how you react and deal with it. Avoid making rash decisions when you're upset or angry; you may regret them later. Be careful about whom you tell, and how much you reveal. Perhaps there's been a misunderstanding. You and your partner may get back together and then will want to forget the split. If you tell your mum they did the dirty on you, she'll still be holding it against them at your Golden Wedding.

Be honest with yourself. It's easy to blame everything on your partner, but if you were partly to blame you need to examine your own conduct. How did something that was so good in the beginning go so wrong? You need to know. Make a list of good and bad points in the relationship, and remember you can discuss these with Marriage Care or Relateline (see Help section). And if you're feeling really low, don't be afraid to talk to your doctor. He or she will understand. Doctors have rocky relationships too.

B

Even if you've been expecting it, the first 24 hours after a break-up are traumatic. If it's happened unexpectedly, it's even worse. You will be shocked, unable to believe that someone who has been part of your life is part of it no longer. You may be so shocked that you're on autopilot, unable to think clearly or plan ahead. And if it was you who called time, you may be battling guilt. A recent survey revealed that men fare less well than women after divorce. However well they hide it, they suffer as much or more in emotional terms than women, often let themselves go, and don't eat properly. And a year after divorce, 48 per cent of men admitted to being 'very lonely', as compared with 35 per cent of women. Women cope better domestically, and also benefit from a greater ability to express their feelings. Poor men, we expect them to maintain a permanent stiff upper lip. Happily, both men and women can turn to organisations such as Relate and Marriage Care if they need support after break-up.

B

In the immediate aftermath there are some don'ts:

1. Don't turn to the bottle.

2. Don't ring round all your friends.

3. If possible, don't tell your family. If the relationship gets back on track (and many do), you may forgive him or her, but they won't.

4. If you want to talk it through and there's no friend you can really trust, ring a helpline (see Help section).

5. Pamper yourself.

6. Don't make any decisions bigger than what to have for lunch.

7. Don't ring the ex and plead for another chance.

8. If you do talk with someone, don't bad-mouth your ex. These things get around and can cause trouble if there's a reconciliation. It could also lead to a tit-for tat, which helps no one at all.

Eventually you will feel restored and ready to date again. You'll have completed the process of dividing possessions, perhaps giving back the ring and, if it applies, the all-important question of custody of the pet. In that instance, it's the welfare of the animal which must come first. Who can care best for Rover, to whom does Rover give most affection ... try to settle this, above all else, with generosity on both sides. Before you do start to rebuild, make sure you have really let go of your old relationship and examined what part, if any, your own actions played in the break-up. That way you can make sure you don't repeat past mistakes (*see also* Licking Your Wounds and Dumped).

Buying love

It's tempting, when a relationship feels rocky, to try to win your partner round with a gift. Of course, you can get a flash of gratitude for those Louboutin shoes or that monogrammed briefcase, but a flash is all you'll get. Gratitude isn't love, and it seldom lasts. Before you spend money or time on trying to win round a reluctant partner, ask yourself if something you have to pay for is really what you want. Will you be paying in money or time or emotion for the rest of the relationship? Better to cut your losses now, and buy a consolation present for yourself before you look to pastures new (*see also* Dignity).

SHE SAYS: Ask 'Why am I special?' and he'll say, 'Because you're you' – a meaningless answer if I ever heard one. It makes you want to force him to sleep in the shed.

> *HE SAYS: Today's woman may rely on looks to get her to the interview, but it is her intellect that secures her seat on the board. Her ego is more resistant than a man's. She will lie, steal, and cheat where necessary. 'I rule' is lettered through today's female executive like 'Blackpool' is through rock.*

SHE SAYS: Men are born young and most of them die that way, kidding themselves that they are masters of situations that are really conceived and controlled by the woman in their life. Which makes it all the more surprising that, when the occasion demands, they find the courage to acquit themselves like heroes.

> *HE SAYS: One way of spotting an Alpha male is to notice which way he faces in a communal shower. Alphas always face outwards. Nervously facing the wall or hiding under a towel is not for them. They never compare the size of their organ – they know it's twice the size of anyone else's, even if folded in half.*

Charisma aka Charm

Some people have it, some don't. Anyone who could bottle it would become richer than Croesus. So is it possible to acquire charisma? Probably not, but it's worth trying. Charismatic people are, above all, good to be with. They are good conversationalists, but they never pin you down and talk you to death. Making you feel good is the real secret of their charm. That means that you sense they are kind and would not betray you. You can be violently attracted to someone you neither like nor approve of, but that is based on lust. Sexual attraction is part of charisma, but not a dominant part. Charismatics can be beautiful or handsome, but many are neither. There is not a hint of the clone about them. They are essentially one-offs. The sensation they arouse in you is that to be apart from them is to be wasting time.

C

Chemistry

See X-factor

Children

It's possible that your new love has children from a previous relationship. Indeed, you may have children yourself. If you're the one who is having to adapt to children, take it slowly. Don't feel threatened by their presence in your partner's life: they are children, not love-rivals. Don't be tempted to criticise them. He or she may well see their faults but that's different from having them pointed out. Don't feel you're the only one who is uncertain. They will be as wary of you as you are of them. And don't see them as constant reminders of former relationships. At the moment you are simply a friend of their parent. If that role develops into something more, there are plenty of people to offer advice and support (see Help section).

If the child or children in question are yours, don't be defensive. But don't sacrifice your children's interests for fear of offending your lover, either. If he or she doesn't realise that children's welfare is paramount, you need to ask yourself if they're right for you. At first don't encourage your children to see the new arrival in your life as anything other than a friend, one of many. If they get too attached, or begin to think of your lover as a fixture, they may find it difficult if the relationship ends. For that reason, it's better if your partner doesn't sleep over until you are fairly sure the relationship is for keeps. And remember there is help for you too, if you feel you need it (*see* Help section).

Once you feel sure this relationship will last, you need to prepare your child. First, get rid of any guilt you may have: you are not only entitled to a life, you must have one as much for your child's sake as your own. But the way to solve this problem is to see it from the child's point of view. Not only have they had your undivided attention, they regard your house as their territory. Will a stranger coming in take the territory from the child, monopolise you, be horrid to them? You can't blame a child for thinking like this. In order to get that child on your side, you have to calm these fears; but you must also be firm about your rights. If you gave up this partner, you would be bound to feel your child had spoiled your life, and that might show. When the child grew up, they would realise what they had done and perhaps feel guilty about leaving you alone while they pursue their own life.

Ask the child's advice on things, as much as you can, because this will make them feel more grown-up and secure. The main thing is to take it slowly, however much in love you

C

may be. You have been alone a long time, and are bound to be thrilled at this new romance; but play it cool for your child's sake. If your new partner is as nice as you think, he or she will understand and co-operate. Keep the child in the loop about all you do, and don't tell fibs – ever. Discuss the child's future, and how, one day, they will leave you to make their own life although you will always be joined in love. And, whatever the temptation, don't ever say, 'You're a little girl/boy, and I will do what I want.' You and your child are a team. Your happiness depends on your taking that child with you; and, if you and your partner proceed slowly but firmly, you can.

Class divide

In all the best fairy stories, the prince can marry the kitchen maid, and they live happily ever after. If you've seen *My Fair Lady*, didn't you want to believe that Professor Higgins and his Cockney guttersnipe could go hand-in-hand into matrimony? In real life, though, can you date, and perhaps commit, across the class or cultural divide? A study by the University of California revealed that we seek partners whose social desirability matches our own. A 1991 survey of 1,300 married couples found that good-looking people picked good-looking mates, rich men fell for wealthy women, and most couples were in roughly the same age group. Men and women tended to be attracted to people with a similar level of education and appreciation of the arts, but when it came to status men cared less about their partner's standing than women did.

Sometimes, however, X-factor takes control, and apparently mismatched couples fall in love. In the beginning, differences can be attractive, even fascinating. The convent-educated girl will be impressed by her macho market-trader. The Eton toff will enjoy 'educating' his shop-girl, and introducing her to the finer things of life. And for both sexes there can be a whiff of danger about venturing outside the usual boundaries. But can it really work? If there is enough love on both sides, along with an appreciation of the inevitable problems, yes it can. But don't underestimate those problems. Family and friends may be openly disapproving. There may be resentment, not only that you have strayed out of your class, but that you have dared to bring an outsider into their charmed circle. And although you may be at home at the opera or a soirée, your partner may feel an inferiority that can turn into resentment towards you for putting them in that position. One thing is certain, the couple who can overcome barriers of education and social standing have a deep and abiding love, and that augurs well for the future.

C

Ten Cheesy Chat-up Lines
(we don't recommend their use)

1. I lost my phone number. Can I borrow yours?
2. I hope you know CPR because you take my breath away.
3. Nice suit . . . I could hang it on my bedroom floor.
4. Remember my name – you'll be screaming it later.
5. I must be lost. I thought Paradise was down south.
6. Let me introduce myself. I'm your future husband.
7. Do you have a pound coin? I need to call my mother and tell her I've met the man of my dreams.
8. Do your legs ache? You've been running through my mind all night.
9. Have you heard about the Modern Alphabet? U and I are in it together.
10. I'm a man, you're a woman. Think of the possibilities.

Commitment

Freedom is the thing we all prize. Commitment should never mean surrendering freedom. It does mean that some decisions will, in future, be taken jointly: it should not mean you have to ask permission to breathe. It does mean you have someone else to consider where before there was only yourself; it also means there is someone to back you. You no longer stand alone, and that 'someone' has your welfare at heart. Consider very carefully before you make your decision, but see commitment, carefully planned, as a door to opportunity, not one that will clang shut upon your liberty. Sometimes people, particularly men, shy away from the responsibility of commitment. Much of the fear of responsibility stems from the old idea that men and men alone were the breadwinners. That idea is misplaced in the modern world. However, there is no doubt that commitment does bring with it a degree of responsibility. Talking together, and outlining how responsibility can be shared should cure most fears. Where someone is truly a commitment-phobe, outside help may be needed (*see* Help section).

Compatibility

In theory, a computer should be able to match anyone with their ideal partner. There would be no need for dating, blind or otherwise, for matchmaking, or all that nonsense – just a click of the mouse and you'd be perfectly paired off. Except that it doesn't work. There's that mysterious thing, X-factor, for a start. And sexual attraction, and a few dozen other things that are part of the magic mix. I believe that shared interests,

C

something computer dating is big on, are not that important. You can have a wonderfully fulfilling relationship without sharing your partner's obsessions, as long as you are both tolerant of the other's needs and desires. What I think is essential to a good relationship is shared standards. Defining shared standards is not easy: a vegetarian can be happy with a non-vegetarian, a Christian with an atheist, as long as there is mutual tolerance. Lovers can disagree about blood sports or politics, even about the death penalty. There are some things, however, on which, to be truly happy, you must be at one. Here is a list of questions you might care to share.

1. How do you feel about money and security?
2. How do you feel about sex?
3. How important to you is your career?
4. Do children figure in your future?
5. What does leisure mean to you?
6. How important to you are friends and family?
7. Do you prize honesty above all else?
8. What are your views on race, religion, and the sanctity of human life?

If the answer to 1 is that you worry intensely about money and security, ask yourself if you could be happy with someone who doesn't care about cash and lives for today. If there is X-factor, or if both of you are prepared to amend your views, a happy relationship might well be possible, but you need to think carefully about things.

If your answer to 2 is that sex is all-important, you need a partner who considers sex as a vital part of union. The twice-a-day lover can accommodate to twice a week, but asking him or her to accept once if there's an R in the month is asking too much. The dedicated career woman will not make a stay-at-home wife, nor will the obsessive careerist satisfy a woman who wants to share everything, including the chores. Again, X-factor can overcome all obstacles, but where there are huge differences you need it in spades. I've lost count of the letters I've had from people who agreed to stay childless at the start of a relationship, and then, as the end of fertility loomed, suddenly realised that a child of their own was all-important – and I'm not just talking about women. The man or woman who likes to socialise will find it difficult to accommodate the partner whose idea of bliss is to spend every evening with their loved one by their own fireside.

The same thing applies to family. If you adore parents, siblings, even distant cousins, beware the potential partner who wants a one-to-one relationship in which outsiders, even family, only figure on the Christmas-card list. And if you can't bear to swat a fly, can you live with someone whose idea of pleasure is a day on the moors with a gun?

C

Where human nature is concerned, there are no unbreakable rules, but allowing lust to overcome common sense is not a good idea. Hopefully you are entering into a relationship that will last. Thinking it through beforehand is the wise thing to do. And a survey in America in 2001 showed that careful preparation for marriage meant a 31 per cent decline in the possibility of divorce.

Compliments

Nothing warms the heart as much as a compliment, but be sparing with them. If you shower them around like rain, they cease to have meaning. Coming occasionally, and only when they are deserved, they work wonders. And don't despise a simple, 'Thank you.' Said with meaning when a lover has been kind or thoughtful, that word can be as effective as a Shakespeare sonnet.

Confession

Confession is often seen as a virtuous action, a cleansing of the soul. Sometimes it is just that – for instance, where you ensure that another person isn't blamed for your wrong action. But there are times when clearing your own conscience can ruin someone else's life, and then confession is not virtuous, it is selfish. If, for example, you have had a fling you deeply regret, the urge to confess and relieve your guilt may be overwhelming. But what will the effect be on a trusting partner? Something akin to a nuclear explosion, perhaps! Keeping your secret is the way you can atone for your mistake, always providing that your remorse is genuine and you will never err again. If you tell, it won't end with your confession and your partner's loving forgiveness. That happens only in fiction. You may be forgiven initially, but then the doubts and the questions will start. 'Was I not enough for you?' 'How is he/she better than me?' and, inevitably 'How can I trust you now?' You have eased your conscience at the expense of your partner's happiness.

Don't imagine I'm advocating lying as an acceptable way to behave. What I am suggesting is that, sometimes, the other person's interests demand your silence. Living with your guilt is the price you are paying for betraying your partner's trust.

Confrontation

When we lose our temper and temperatures rise, we need an outlet. An outburst can give us that opportunity to let off steam, but it's not always a good idea. It can give you a moment's

C

satisfaction, and 24 hours of grief. When we get angry we tend to stop up our ears and eyes, and cease to listen to or observe the other person. Words well up, and get said when they might have been better left unsaid. Our anger makes the other person feel defensive, and get angry in return. They're not listening to what we're saying, so we can end up shouting one another down. Yes, there's always the chance that charging in with guns blazing can get you a result, but it's more likely that a calm discussion would have achieved a better one. A big row can sometimes result in lifelong enmity. Better to turn someone who annoyed you into a friend if you can.

If you must have a row, stay calm. The old adage of counting to ten before you speak can be quite useful. If possible, discuss the problem beforehand with a sensible friend, someone who won't just agree with everything you say and urge you on. Try to see the other person's point of view, because understanding where they're coming from makes it easier to defeat them.

Don't drag in side issues ... yes, they forgot your birthday the year before last, but how is that relevant now? Stick to the point. It can help to write down your case beforehand so that it's clear in your mind. Above all, think and rethink whether or not confrontation is a good idea. If, after reflection, you decide it is the only way, then stick to your guns until you win the argument (*see also* Arguments).

Contraception

It's important that you have faith in whatever form of contraception you're using. You should be able to discuss this with your partner, because he or she needs security too. Talk to your doctor or consult the Family Planning Association. They will advise you of the form most suitable for you. You can choose between the pill or an intra-uterine device. The sheath is a third option, and there are other, more invasive techniques. It's important that you know that no contraceptive is 100-per-cent effective, although some are a great deal more reliable than others. Get good advice, so that you can enter into a sexual relationship with the easy mind essential to true fulfilment. Termination is always a possibility, but it doesn't come without a lot of heart-searching (see Termination). A baby is for ever, and nothing else is capable of providing as much entertainment, pride, worry or bafflement. But entered into by accident, pregnancy can be a headache like no other. Think before you risk conception.

Controlling

It begins so gently, perhaps with a request to wear a particular item of clothing 'because I like it on you'. Or to cut or not cut your hair. After that, just a suggestion that a little less of your

C

friends would be welcome. Then it's a little frown each time you suggest seeing your mum. Bit by bit you are discouraged from seeing the people who made up your old life. In return you'll be loved, cosseted, and treated like a prince or princess. Don't let this fool you: you are in the hands of a control freak, and slowly but surely your partner will wall you up in the little cell they have constructed for you. Don't let it happen. The love they are prepared to lavish on you once they have isolated you is a perverted kind of love that can quite easily turn to icy contempt. Get out while you can.

If you need encouragement, ring Women's Aid or Men's Advice Line (see Help section), where advice is available for both homosexual and heterosexual relationships.

Crazy

Just occasionally, that great guy or gal who can be enormous fun will go too far. Suddenly the fun isn't fun at all. Deep down you're scared. Don't ignore that fear and tell yourself that they are just high-spirited and will settle down in time. They well may.

You may also be in the hands of a crazy. Don't keep hoping the problem will go away. Seek advice now (*see* Help section). Perhaps the relationship is over, but they won't

C

accept it. Perhaps they bombard you with texts and emails, turn up at your place of work, are waiting in the door to your block of flats. If a polite request to leave you alone doesn't work, seek help. If you're scared, contact the police, or consult the Help section.

Crushes

See Unrequited Love

SHE SAYS: Let's hear no more of 'It's a guy thing,' or 'Women are like that.' Those phrases are simply excuses for bad behaviour.

> *HE SAYS: I don't Google much since I got married. The wife knows everything.*

SHE SAYS: 'Your guess is as good as mine,' means 'Why the hell should I explain?' and suggests he's pissed-off. 'Fine,' means 'not fine at all'– unless it's said absent-mindedly while he's trying to unhook your bra.

> *HE SAYS: Women ask, 'Is everything OK?' You say 'Fine', which seems a perfectly straightforward word to me. Does it satisfy them? Does it hell! 'What do you mean by fine? Finer than you felt before? Finer than it was with her? I mean, fine is fine. If it wasn't fine, you'd be out of there.*

SHE SAYS: Men (unless they're habitual liars) behave as if God only gave them so many words, and they have to save some for their old age.

D

Dance classes

These are rapidly becoming one of the best ways of having a night out, and making friends of both sexes into the bargain. But too many people are scared of venturing through the door, never mind on to the floor. By far and away the hardest step in any form of social dancing, be it salsa, tango, or ballroom, is that first one through the door. Most beginners are terrified of it, and their fears are misguided.

D

♥ If you turn up at the start of the nigh,t the assumption will be you have never danced before.

♥ It is highly unlikely you will be the only beginner there.

♥ The first thing that will happen is that you will be shown how to dance some basic steps by an experienced instructor, firstly in a line and then with a partner. You do not need to take a partner, everyone will dance with each other, changing intermittently at the instructor's request. This will allow you to get to know the other dancers there.

♥ Don't worry that anyone will be looking at you. You will be too wrapped up in your own steps to worry about anyone else . . . and so will they.

♥ Most experienced dancers will be willing to help you out; this is generally encouraged by most, if not all, clubs. Most experienced dancers remember when someone was kind enough to help them.

♥ Later in the evening there will be a more advanced class which you can watch and eventually participate in as your confidence and ability increase.

D

Anyone who can dance well will have passed through several stages including 'Can dance a bit' and prior to that 'Absolutely hopeless'. 'Absolutely hopeless' is a dumb phrase to use at any time. You wouldn't say you were 'absolutely hopeless' at ice skating, though you might say you couldn't do it because you'd never tried it and hadn't had any lessons. So it is with dancing: you can't say how good or how hopeless you are until you try. Today's dance classes understand that.

A lot of people are afraid of looking foolish when they first start dancing. But anyone who can dance well is unlikely to consider your virginal moves with scorn – they can all remember their own first shaky experiences on the dance floor, and most good dancers are more than willing to help nervous beginners. Some venues supply experienced partners whose job is solely to help newcomers. After this first lesson, there is usually some free dancing to music before another more advanced lesson for the experienced dancers; and finally the rest of the night is your own. It is generally considered bad form to refuse a dance; all you're asking or asked for is one dance, not a quick gambol through the more taxing parts of the Kama Sutra. It is probably best to start off with a popular form of dancing: salsa, ceroc, ballroom etc. (the internet will provide you with local details).

The advantage of a well-attended class is that it will have a good selection of dancers of differing abilities, and if it's

D

popular that's probably because it's well run — that is to say, friendly, with well taught classes (often with visiting guest teachers) and good music. Dancing is nature's own Prozac: it will keep you fit, keep your brain active, increase your social circle immensely, and on a good night will make you feel as high as a giraffe in an air balloon. You'll meet people from both sexes and all walks of life. Once you can dance a little, you can go almost anywhere in the modern world. You walk into a club and know a whole bunch of people by the time you leave, which is a boon. Everyone was a beginner once — so what are you waiting for?

Dartboard

I have seen so many potentially good relationships founder because one partner or the other was too impatient that I have evolved a theory. It's called the Dartboard. Imagine a dartboard. A couple enter the outer ring together on a first date. The bull's eye is total commitment. Ideally they will move hand in hand through the various rings, until they reach the bull's eye together and, by mutual consent, are in a lasting relationship. All too often, however, one partner, usually but not always the woman, wants to speed through the rings to the bull's eye. The other person takes fright at this too-rapid

D

1st ring
You are entitled only to courtesy. The other person may or may not contact you again. If he or she is seeing others, that is their right.

2nd ring
You meet their friends. You expect to be contacted again.

3rd ring
You meet family. At this stage, although the other person may still have friends of both sexes, they don't go on 'dates'. You may buy one another small gifts.

4th ring
You talk of the future. You are known as his/her other half. You have a right to know what is going on in his/her life. You may reveal some or all of your past.

5th ring
Bull's eye: commitment. You make plans, perhaps move in together, and set dates.

Dartboard 55

D

pace, and backs off. The relationship is over when, if the impatient one had simply waited, they might have achieved that all important goal, commitment.

So what do you have a right to expect as a relationship grows? When should you be introduced to friends? To family? When should you be the only man/woman in your opposite number's life? When should there be talk of a future together? As to the question of when sex should occur, there is no fixed answer, although sex on that outer ring is not advisable (see below). How long you should stay in each ring is a matter of individual choice. For some people the progression from outer ring to bull's eye will take six months, for others three years or more. The accompanying illustration is not a suggestion of the speed at which things should go, rather a suggestion of progress.

You will notice there is no mention of sex in any ring. That is because sex is such a personal issue that its timing cannot be decided by a rule. People are different, and allow others into their lives at different paces. For some it may occur early, even in the first ring. Others will be more cautious. However, the fact that your relationship is now a sexual one is not a guarantee of permanence, and you would be unwise to think it so. That is one reason for delaying sexual intercourse until other factors have shown that this relationship is more than a casual one.

D

Dating

See also Meeting

Blind dates: Most of us have friends who say, 'I know just the man/woman for you.' They may be right but the probability is they're not. How many of us have endured a ghastly evening trying to make conversation with someone who is clearly as disappointed in you as you are in them? Should you turn down every blind date which is offered? No, because it may be your Dream Lover they have lined up. However, don't build up your hopes; whatever your degree of disappointment, be unfailingly kind and courteous to your date; and don't leave them with false hopes. 'I'm going to be fearfully busy for the next few months, but I've enjoyed tonight, and hopefully our paths will cross at some time in the future,' is a polite way of saying, 'Not again' without being too cruel. And always make sure to go Dutch. If you don't, you may feel obliged to issue an invitation just so you can return the obligation.

Internet dating: More than 8 million people in the UK use the internet for dating. It's quick and easy, sometimes too easy. There are 1400 dating websites in Britain and 16 million single people. Surveys suggest that more than a third of them

D

have tried internet dating to one extent or another. The fact that you're chatting with someone while sitting in your own home can give a false sense of security, so be careful. However, it's a means of meeting a large number of people who are also looking for a partner. You can do it from home, and if you strike up a good conversation with someone it builds confidence. It can be easier to be more relaxed and honest when you are in front of a screen, but always remember that there may be people out there who exploit this (*see* Romance Fraud).

You need to be cautious, and keep your wits about you. People can lie on the internet, and you might find out the person you've been happily chatting to is a teenager out for a laugh at someone's expense. There are also people who are looking for casual sex or extra-marital encounters, so be aware of this, and don't let yourself get hurt emotionally by getting involved with someone too soon. But, equally, don't imagine that everyone out there is necessarily a fraud. They may be like you, entirely sincere.

D

Here are some tips for successful dating on the internet:

- Don't tell fibs but don't be over-modest. Ask a truthful friend to help you list your good points.

- People are seven times more likely to look at profiles with photos, but pick one which is realistically you. That will save disappointment later.

- Don't be too definite about what you want. If you say you're looking for short-term relationships, it can suggest that you simply want a fling. If you say you want long-term commitment people will hear the prison doors closing behind them.

- Choose your sites carefully. Paying for a professional one can be pricy, but at least you know that the people on it will be serious. The internet is full of jokers.

- Look at sites aimed at hobbies you already have, or those you think you might enjoy if you tried them. That way you'll be meeting someone with the same interests.

- Chat on the phone, or use a web-cam, but be careful about people seeking inappropriate images.

- Some sites offer a free trial to prospective members, so this is a good way to try them out if you're not sure.

- Social networking sites are another way of expanding your circle of friends, but, again, proceed with caution.

D

As with any form of dating, be careful when you meet people. Ten to one you're meeting a good guy or gal, but much better be safe than sorry. Always arrange to meet in a public place, and if possible, ask a friend to be at a distance at the meeting. You could even pretend to bump into them, and introduce them to your date. If that's not possible, give a friend information about your date and where and when you are meeting. Don't be afraid to cut things short if you feel uncomfortable. And if, at any stage, there is a request for money, cease contact *immediately*.

What are the chances of finding lasting romance on the internet? Some sites will claim a one-in-500 chance of marriage, but they don't tell you how many frogs you'd have to meet or how long you'd have to be a member before you found your prince. I would never rule it out altogether, but I'd strongly suggest you don't choose it as your only method of looking for love.

Singles' events: Your local reference library should have details of local events. See also Help section for national singles organisations.

Speed-dating: You have three to five minutes to chat to several men or women, so the advantages are that you'll meet a large number of people in one evening. Events are usually

D

held in a bar or club. It can be quite tiring, because you have to try to impress people in a very short time, and make conversation with lots of people as well as trying to remember the names of people you'd like to talk to again. If you approach it in the right frame of mind, though, it can be great fun. You don't have to make instant decisions because the organiser will arrange for you to contact anyone who has impressed you.

Here are some tips for successful speed-dating:

♥ Make sure you wear something you feel comfortable in, and choose a colour you like and know suits you.

♥ Gen up on the latest news and current affairs, and, if you're in a town or village, keep up with local news, too.

♥ Think of some questions to ask people beforehand.

♥ If possible, go with friends to make it a fun evening, whatever the outcome.

♥ Don't take it too seriously, and aim to have fun.

D

Dinner parties, arranged by a singles' organisation, where you'll meet around ten to 15 people, can be a pleasant way of making new friends. These can be good value, because you'll meet a lot of people in one evening, and have a nice meal. And meeting in a group like that takes the pressure off a bit (see Help section).

Singles' holidays: The thought of going on holiday alone can be terrifying, especially if you've never been on holiday on your own before. However, travel companies now realise how many single people holiday, and they can cater for every need. These days you'll find a wide range of fun holidays that won't cost you the earth and will widen your circle of acquaintances. You're likely to make some friends, and enjoy the trip into the bargain. You can opt for short breaks or long-haul holidays; you'll have a tour manager to oversee things; and some agencies don't charge single supplements. It can be a good way to boost your confidence because you know the holiday will come to an end eventually, and that can give you a sense of freedom. You can take part in a huge range of activities, including adventure or hobby holidays, and you'll be meeting other people with the same interests and developing your skills at the same time.

Trips that require you to be energetic, such as a walking or mountain trekking, will not only improve your circle of friends, they'll make you fitter – and if you tone up first at the gym, that's another source of friendship. If activity is not your

D

bag, there are holidays with the emphasis on history or the arts, or simply having fun. Ask around and hear what friends and acquaintances have to say about their experiences, and don't be afraid to question your travel agents.

Dating agencies: There are agencies catering for every kind of client. You get the benefit of a personal touch, and things are organised for you, so you feel more relaxed. Most agencies guarantee a set number of dates, and it can feel safer as you know that each person you meet has been vetted by the agency. Another advantage is that they select who you meet. You may be surprised to find that you hit it off with someone you would not have picked out yourself. The downside is the cost, and the fact that you don't know how much attention to detail goes into the matching process. If you are considering using an agency, go for one that is vetted by the Association of British Introduction Agencies (ABIA). Better still, use one recommended by someone who found it helpful.

Classified ads: These are cheap, if a little cheesy. You write a brief description of what you're looking for, and people contact you, usually by leaving a message on a voicemail box, which can give you some idea of what they're like. Unlike the internet, there won't be a photo, which means you won't be put off a potential soul-mate because they don't look like the

D

man or woman of your dreams. Ads tend to be quite short, and use a peculiar shorthand, so browse the columns before you write your own. Words such as 'genuine' or 'humorous' go down well, but if you can add a little something quirky it will make your ad stand out. As with internet dating, or indeed any other form of introduction, use your common sense, and be cautious when meeting for the first time. Chatting online or on the phone can build up a sense of expectation, and the feeling that you know a person. This can lead to disappointment when you meet them in the flesh, and spoil what, taken more slowly, might have been a good relationship (*see also* Dance Classes: one of the best ways of meeting people).

However strong the attraction when you do meet, don't jump into bed with someone straight away. It might seem like a good idea at the time, but the strong possibility is that you'll regret it afterwards. It can also create a wrong impression which will be difficult to erase. Get to know each other as friends first, and see if you are as compatible in real life as you were on the web. Whatever you do, you should always practise safe sex.

Before the meeting, make an effort with your appearance. Pay attention to detail – your hands and nails, unladdered tights, or clean jeans. Little things send a message to someone else about your sense of self-worth. More importantly, they up that self-worth. Make the effort to look good at all times, not just on special occasions – you never

D

know who you might bump into, and it's good for your morale, anyway. Looking good, which is not the same thing as being dressed up, will boost your self-esteem, and give you the confidence to talk to other people. You don't have to spend a lot of money – it's more about your style, and the effort you put into life.

Develop your small talk for that first meeting (see Small Talk). Don't feel you have to impress, but showing that you're up on the news of the day can help. Don't be scared to talk about yourself, but don't make it your sole topic of conversation. Ask questions, but keep them fairly casual. 'Do you work around here?' or 'Do you come from this part of the world?' will do for starters, and give the other person something they will find easy to talk about. Pay attention to what they say, but don't give the impression you're hanging on their every word. Don't be afraid of the occasional silence, and don't forget to smile occasionally. Above all, remember that they're just as anxious as you are, and possibly more so.

If you're meeting someone you've met through the internet or contact sites, be sure to stay safe. Always tell a friend where you are going, and with whom, giving telephone numbers and addresses where possible. Meet people in the daytime if possible, and in public places. And be equally cautious on second dates. The time will come when you can relax but it's not yet.

D

Don't approach a date as an ordeal. At worst it will be a wasted evening, at best the start of something good. Don't allow huge expectations; nothing worth while comes easily, except in romantic novels.

Chances are tonight won't bring you the lover of your dreams, but out of a string of such encounters something good may grow. And remember: he or she probably shares your trepidation, so put them at their ease by showing an interest in their life and views. Above all, don't cherish an ideal and therefore turn down anyone who doesn't, at first sight, fit the mould. Inside unprepossessing boxes magic delights may lurk.

Depression

What is depression? It's a state of unhappiness that is having a detrimental effect on your life. We all get the blues, a low mood that lasts for a while and is gone. Depression is a deep feeling of misery that persists and needs professional help from your doctor. A recent study shows that a third of women have taken anti-depressants. The figure for men is lower, but that is probably owing to male reluctance to seek help. The likelihood is that a high proportion of that depression was due to relationship problems.

D

Many people are afraid of anti-depressants. 'They're addictive,' they say, or 'I'll be a zombie.' In fact, anti-depressants properly prescribed and taken for a short period, can give you the strength to sort out your problems and get your life back on track. If you want to keep prescribed drugs as a last resort, Omega 3 fatty acids have been shown to help depression, and you find them in oily fish, nuts, seeds, and dark-green vegetables. Alternatively, you can buy Omega 3 capsules. Vitamin D, the sunshine vitamin can help too, so get out into the sunshine when you can.

Insomnia is a side-effect of depression, and a hot, milky drink at bedtime supplies magnesium, which inhibits the stress hormone, cortisol. Exercise is helpful for mild to moderate depression; and St John's Wort is often recommended as a herbal remedy. I would always consult your doctor before taking St John's Wort. If depression refuses to budge, turn to a sympathetic ear. Relate will understand and help you see that the end of a relationship is not the end of happiness but merely a hiccup on the way. If it's something else that has brought you down, you'll find sources of support in the Help section.

D

Dignity

Whatever else you lose, hang on to your dignity. It's something that no lover, no spiteful enemy, no unfaithful friend, can take away from you unless you let them. If a lover has betrayed you or dumped you in a callous way, hold your head high. He's the one in the wrong, not you. If gossip hurts you, if people gang up on you online, they are the low life, not you. Where possible, don't respond; but if you think you have been legally wronged take advice. On the whole, however, I think it's better to rise above these situations, and let your detractors mess about in the gutter where they belong. They want you to respond. Faithless lovers like nothing better than hearing that you are broken-hearted without them. Deny them that pleasure, and move on.

D

Domestic violence

No one would willingly enter into an abusive relationship. The trouble is that an abusive relationship doesn't come with a warning ticket. It creeps up on you. A clever abuser will break down your defences inch by inch so that, when real abuse occurs, you have no resistance. Nor is the abuser always male: women are just as capable of bringing a partner to his knees, and there has been a rise in the number of male victims in the past few years.

It begins so slowly. Little comments that shake your self-esteem. 'Is it time to get your roots done?' 'I'm not sure you can wear jeans.' These are harmless in themselves, but are designed to make you start to feel undesirable. To destroy your sense of self-worth, so that you will stay with the abuser, whatever happens, because if you went who else would love you? And although you know you should turn to family and friends, you don't because, first, your partner has managed to banish them from your life, and second, even if friends were there you'd be too embarrassed to speak out. And all the while there's this voice in your head that says, 'You must have done something to deserve this.'

Even if the abuse is non-violent, it is destructive. Sometimes mental abuse can be worse than the physical variety.

D

Here are some facts about DV:

♥ It constitutes a quarter of all violent crime in the UK.

♥ There have usually been 30 or more incidents before the police become involved.

♥ It claims the lives of two women a week, and 30 men a year.

One final top tip: does being with your partner make you feel really relaxed, or does it make you feel on edge? If it's the latter, you have thinking to do. See Helplines for people to whom you can talk.

Doubts

Our emotional life and relationships are so important to our well-being that it's natural to have qualms – which is a posh word for doubts. Right up to the altar, you can occasionally wonder if you're doing the right thing. The question is, do you regard your doubts as a warning that you should change course, or are they simply a sign that you're a bit insecure and inclined to fear decision-making? When you first feel there's something special about a relationship you can start to wonder: are we compatible? Will it last? Does he/she mean what they say? Your list of doubts can be endless. You need an impartial opinion, and sometimes you can get that from a friend or family member. You need to be cautious, however, because if news of your doubts get back to your significant other, there could be trouble. Better, probably, to talk them over with a dispassionate third party, someone who doesn't have anything to gain by pushing you in one direction or another. Relate or Marriage Care will help with any relationship problem (see Help section).

Dream lover

Although *One Day*, the best-selling novel by David Nicholls, would have us believe there is *the one* out there for each of us, it's not true. Those of us who have loved more than once can testify to that. But it's true that most of us, male and female, do emerge from adolescence with a clear idea of who we want to spend the rest of our lives with. Even when we embark on a satisfying career, the Dream Lover is there at the back of our mind – tall, dark and handsome, or blonde and petite, as the case may be. The trouble is that that vision of a Dream Lover can make you pass over anyone who doesn't resemble the dream. And that's a pity (see Expectations).

D

Drifting apart

Sometimes a relationship which, on paper, is perfect will simply fizzle out. Usually one partner or both are completely ignorant of why. In most cases it turns out they came together impulsively, swept on by a tide of sexual attraction, or because they were simply 'so well matched'. When that wellspring of attraction dries up, they'll say they 'needed something more', but few of them know what that 'something' is. All they know is that they need to get out. What can make the 'getting out' difficult is that your partner may not deserve it. He or she may be giving 100 per cent to the relationship, but if you can't give 100 per cent back you need to take action. Friends and family may find it difficult to understand: 'You're mad,' they may say, because outwardly you seem to have it all. Only you can understand that empty feeling that tells you it's time to go. Years ago there was a stigma attached to walking out on a relationship. Divorce was taboo, and breach-of-promise cases not uncommon. Today we are more sensible: we accept that holding a relationship together when it has run out of steam doesn't benefit anyone. A recent survey of family lawyers revealed that adultery was no longer the principal reason for divorce. Most couples simply stated that they were no longer in love, or had grown apart. As in marriage, so with relationships: they sometimes fracture and fall apart without anyone's being to blame. Sometimes it's possible to restore that binding ingredient, and a counsellor can be helpful here (see Help section). Whether or not it works, it can be helpful in letting your partner see that you didn't walk away without thought or making an effort. And it may help you to recognise that that vision of freedom you found so enticing isn't all it seemed. The important thing is that, if you stay in a relationship, it should be because it's what you really want, and not because you can't face the outcry if you go.

Driving

The car is the perfect arena for a row. Even a sharp intake of breath can arouse anger in the driver. If you're in the passenger seat, know your place: it's not behind the wheel. If your partner's driving gives serious cause for concern, discuss it at a later date, not when he or she should be keeping cool and keeping eyes on the road. Some people are natural drivers, which can make them pretty tetchy passengers. Think twice before you pass comments, and never make jokes about 'dicing with death' and so forth. The choice of a car can be rocky terrain. She wants a comfortable saloon with lots of luggage space. He wants what she will call a penis extension the first time they fall out. If one person is paying for the car,

D

it's their decision. If it's jointly financed, it should be jointly chosen. And there's no point in buying a car which, however lovely its lines, will terrify your partner when it's their turn to drive.

Dumped

It happens to us all at sometime or another and it hurts like hell (see Breaking Up, and also Licking Your Wounds).

D

HE SAYS: There's an immortal line: 'Love means never having to say you're sorry.' Well, immortal it may be, accurate it ain't. Any lover will tell you that grovelling — the art of saying 'Sorry' in 47 languages — is at the heart of any good relationship.

> *SHE SAYS: When it comes to sex, women have not only caught up with men, they've out-classed them. They are bolder, coarser, and keener to state their requirements. It's progress.*

HE SAYS: Women never say what they mean. You spend months, even years, before you unlock the code. For example, 'It doesn't really matter,' actually means 'It matters so much I'll leave you if you don't do it/say it/make it happen.'

> *SHE SAYS: When women feel bad they go shopping. Men invade someone else's country.*

HE SAYS: Sometimes women will use an alternative ploy. They'll be rude to you — really rude.
This is a good sign.

Dumped

SHE SAYS: Men can't find the right words because they can only operate one organ at a time, and the penis wins hands down.

> *HE SAYS: Years ago, men wrote love poems and sentimental letters. They proposed on one knee and likened their women to April skies. Now it's a text message: 'Hope U R on 4 2nite'.*

SHE SAYS: Today's top female will still keep the pantry filled. I factor in the supermarket run alongside meetings and reviews.

> *HE SAYS: ou see a picture of Becks smooth as a baby's bottom, and enrol for a full body wax.*
> *Your eyes water for a week, which is how long it takes the regrowth to start. You contemplate a Brazilian next time, but cry off when you hear you have to bite on a tongue depressor to dull the pain.*

SHE SAYS: When I clutch my Prada, I feel strong.

> *HE SAYS: There are five ways of dating a woman: blind, speed, internet, organised, or random. Random is the one where you fancy the colleague who is so proud of her 40DD cup that she positively flourishes it. You ask if she'd like to go out for a drink, and find yourself facing sexual-harassment charges for eyeing her cleavage.*

Ego

In recent years, the word 'ego' has come to mean something like arrogance or big-headedness. In fact, our ego is an essential part of our being. If it gets too bruised, we retreat into ourselves; so be careful how you treat other people's egos, and protect your own from too much damage. If you come up against an arrogant individual, or one whose every word is a boast, tread carefully. He or she may look and feel good, but living with arrogance is not easy. And who wants to be tied to Mr or Miss Perfect? (*see also* Self-esteem).

Emails

You may think yours is a strong relationship: you feel secure and happy. And then, suddenly, there on your lover's computer

E

is an email, a flirty email, from another man or woman whom you knew nothing about. Someone who obviously knows all about you, and mentions a recent meeting with your partner. Immediately you feel betrayed – but what can you do about it? After all, you shouldn't have been snooping through their emails. (And that's equally true if the rogue message came via a mobile phone.) You can't simply let it go, however, because you feel as though someone has just fired a rocket into your life.

There may be an innocent explanation for the email. Did it come from a work colleague, an old college friend, someone who has been in the background of your partner's life for so long that they've become wallpaper, and that's why he or she never mentioned them? Unless there are specific sexual details in the message, you can't assume they are lovers. On the other hand, the chances of your forgetting this and moving on are nil. You need a conversation with your partner, but that will necessitate revealing that you were snooping in their emails, and they could well accuse you of lack of trust. You have options: you can simply push the whole thing to the back of your mind, and get on with living. You can have an immediate showdown and risk a row that will end in parting. Or you can box clever, say nothing about the email, but be vigilant, particularly about time. Is your partner home on time; do they make excuses to slip away? Are they more sexually affectionate (frequently a sign of guilt); and do they keep their phone by their side at all times? Hopefully there'll be none of these signs, and you can dismiss your suspicions. If there are clues to a liaison, however, at least you have a case to put forward, which is much better than saying, 'I sneaked into your emails.' Perhaps your partner will have a good explanation. If not Relate will help you decide whether or not to stay.

Emails can be dangerous if sent in haste. If you receive an email that angers or upsets you, walk away from your computer and cool down before you answer it. Hurried emails can say more than they should. There should be a sign above every computer saying, 'Retreat and Consider'. Repeated emails can also be irritating. You may have time on your hands, but he or she may be up to their necks in work. Only email when you really have something to say.

Emotional intelligence

Emotional intelligence is one of those phrases we bandy about without, perhaps, fully understanding its meaning. So what is it? Put simply, it's the ability to understand your own feelings, and interpret from their reactions the feelings of others. Some people are born with it. Most of us can acquire some of it, often through painful experience. The reason why

E

it is to be valued is that, if you have it, it enables you to work out what is going on in other people's minds, and guide your own behaviour accordingly. Once you understand why your lover is sad, you know how to comfort them. If you understand why they're angry, and whether you are the cause of their anger, or whether some outside factor caused it, you are half-way to defusing that anger. That's why it's worth trying to understand emotional intelligence. Two experts, Salovey and Mayer, identified four different factors of emotional intelligence: the perception of emotion, the ability to reason using emotions, the ability to understand emotion, and the ability to manage emotions. If that sounds too technical, it simply amounts to learning what makes you and others tick.

Engagement

The moment when the ring goes on your or your beloved's finger should be a happy one. It's the official sign that you two belong together. Too often, nowadays, it's followed by endless list-making, frightening expense, rows over bridesmaids or best men, and a general lessening of that first happy euphoria. Be careful that that doesn't happen to you.

E

Engaged forever?

Some people are quite happy to enter into an engagement, but there the commitment ends. Somehow there's never a good time to go that one important step further and make the relationship legal. There will be excuses: finishing a work issue; getting promotion; being in a position to afford children; breaking the news to exes or children of a previous relationship; and the *big* one, the cost. The last one is the phony, because a wedding needn't break the bank unless you want it to. Whatever the excuses, if you feel there'll only ever be one ring on your finger and it isn't a wedding ring, set a discussion date by mutual agreement. Be generous: you have waited this long, so another six months won't hurt. But when that discussion comes, it must end with you either setting the date officially, or with you recognising that you're at a dead end, and moving on.

Erotic capital

Erotic capital is simply a way of describing making the best of yourself. Men and women who wanted to get ahead or attract the opposite sex have always done it. Knowing you look your best can make an enormous difference, so doing your best to

E

make the most of your assets is to be praised. The danger comes when the way you look becomes over-important to you. Obsession with your appearance is unattractive. Yes, looking like a model can bring potential lovers flocking to you, or get you that promotion, but if lovers or employers find little or nothing under that glossy exterior, if your capital is nothing more than appearance – they will soon lose interest. And if you can't appear in public because you've broken a fingernail you have problems.

So, assess what you have going for you and maximise your good points, by all means. Just make sure that appearance is only part of what you have to offer. Lots of people who could not be described as beautiful, handsome, or fashionable make fulfilling, lasting relationships, or make it to the boardroom.

Exes

If you've had a long relationship with someone, affection can remain even after a split. Sometimes this can lead to sex, which may even be better once the strain of the relationship is removed. This can be dangerous, though, because it can remind you only of the good parts of being together, the passion and the fulfilment. You need to remind yourself exactly why you left, and put some space between you, if you

E

can. It may also mean that one partner is simply using the other, and when that becomes apparent it's demeaning. Many people do regret ending the relationship: four out of ten people surveyed regretted divorcing, but that can often be owing to rose-coloured spectacles. Take a good look at the life you had together. Make a list of pros and cons, and examine the reason why it ended.

Another danger area can be an obsession with your current lover's ex. You want to whisper, 'Was it better with her/him?' after sex; you cringe if you come across a photo, or his or her name crops up in conversation. In fact, the threat to your relationship comes not from the ex but from your own lack of self-esteem. You will become increasingly needy, always begging for reassurance, and that's a drag. You may find yourself provoking rows because you want him or her to demonstrate their love for you, even when you're being beastly. Turn to the section on Self-esteem, and then consider whether or not talking to Relate could help (*see* Help section).

E

Expectations

Look at all the lonely-hearts columns and you'll realise that most people have a picture of how their dream lover will be. Almost every female ad will specify 'tall', and men will say 'slim'. Both sexes want someone with a 'GSOH'. Few are sordid enough to mention money, but a lot say 'professional preferred', in the hope of high salaries. Some say 'interest in sport' or 'theatre', because they don't want to give up their own interests. Advertising themselves, they're obviously aware of what the other person will be looking for, and try to satisfy it, whether or not they're telling the truth. In fact, their dream lover, the one who can transport them to undreamed-of delights, may be right in front of them. The trouble is, he may be short and work blue-collar. She may be slightly overweight and know nothing at all about sport. So their soulmate will pass them by for no other reason than that their wrapping paper is the wrong colour.

Even if you do find your tall, professional GSOH, you may find that, underneath the shiny cover, they're not what you wanted at all. Moral: take a good look at all the goods. Under a plain cover might lurk a pleasant surprise.

E

SHE SAYS: Driving you to his place or yours does not count as foreplay.

> *HE SAYS: Today, with women putting everything in the shop window, a man's groin is activated hourly — which is why we haven't discovered anything much since the bagless vacuum cleaner.*

SHE SAYS: When it comes to sex women have not only caught up with men, they've out-classed them. They are bolder, coarser and keener to state their requirements. The last woman to lie back and think of England was Margaret Thatcher, and she was coming from a different viewpoint.

> *SHE SAYS: Ask for reassurance and all you get is 'I'm not the romantic type', or even worse, 'You know I can't say things like that'.*
> *Well, yes he can. He has a tongue. He thinks. He can say 'Will you iron my rugby shirt?' quick enough.*

HE SAYS: Real mates don't fight over women. By the time you've sunk a couple of pints it's settled and you toss for who'll tell her she's on her own. No woman's worth the loss of a mate.

Expectations

HE SAYS: I'm not privy to what goes on in the ladies' loo, but anyone who thinks men don't compare notes is seriously ill-informed.

> *SHE SAYS: Once upon a time being a woman was simple. All you had to do was be nice, look nice, talk nice, cook nice, and you'd be kept for life. Thank God it's changed.*

HE SAYS: Being a man used to be simple. You had to be hard: work hard, play hard, display no emotion unless in the total darkness of the marital bedroom, and you would reap the rewards of being proper man. It's different now.

> *SHE SAYS: Men's faces improve with sleep. They look like little boys when they wake, even with stubble. Women's faces disintegrate, and even if you cleansed the night before, little rings of yesterday's mascara make you look like a lemur. At times like that you want to be alone.*

HE SAYS: Why do women keep asking you if they look all right? Any fool could work out that if they looked like a dog, you'd be long gone.

86 The A to Z of Love, Sex and Exasperation

Fairy tales

Fairy tales have their place, but it's at children's bedtimes. They seldom happen in real life, and living in the expectation of one coming true for you is a waste of time. That said, there's a prince or princess in each one of us, so two people can turn an everyday romance into a fairy tale if they really want to.

Faking

Most women will confess to faking orgasm occasionally, usually because they're desperate for sleep. More than half (53.9%) of 453 heterosexual women questioned in the United States admitted to faking with their current partner. Until recently, no one discussed male faking, but that happens. If faking happens occasionally it's harmless, but if it's regular you need help (see Help section).

F

Fantasy

It's difficult to put a figure on how many people fantasise during sex, but it is probable that most people do, to one extent or another. Sometimes they confide their guilt: 'I love my husband, so why do I have to pretend I'm being ravaged by a highwayman/Brad Pitt/my doctor?' 'Why do I need to think Angelina Jolie is standing over me with a whip?' Whatever turns you on, is the answer. Having a fantasy lover doesn't mean you don't love the real live man or woman in your bed. You're using the fantasy as a trigger to help towards release, so fantasise away without fearing damage to your relationship. Unless, that is, you confide your fantasy to your lover. Some men or women will leap at the chance to fulfil your desires, if they're capable of fulfilment. Most of them will be disappointed to learn that they're not your fantasy. So best keep your secret lover to yourself.

Sometimes the fantasy can be an extension of something in the past, something almost fearful. If your fantasy is disturbing rather than pleasurable, consider talking to one of Relate's therapists. A fantasy can feature leather, bondage, or domination. Although about 10 per cent of the population is believed to engage in bondage and domination, it's likely that twice that number use it as a fantasy. That's where fantasies are useful, indulging your imagination without fear of harm.

F

Father/mother figures

There are times in our lives when we all want to be fussed over, to be mummy's pet or daddy's little girl for few moments. If you have the uneasy feeling that your lover is really looking for a mum or dad substitute, you have some thinking to do. There will be times when you need to lean on someone: will the person who demands you cosset them give you the support you need when that time comes? A good relationship is one between equals. If you feel junior tugging at your skirts or trouser leg, think very carefully.

Flirting

Kept within bounds, flirting is good for you – and probably for whoever you're flirting with. It's that extra smile or twitch of the lips, that widening of the eyes, that dropping of the voice, that well-manicured finger on your wrist – it's harmless, and it can happen between people of all ages. It's harmless because everyone concerned knows there is no end-product to it. If flirting gets out of hand, if you are deliberately leading someone on with the unspoken promise of an end-product, then unless it is happening between two people who have no ties and are free to come together, it is dangerous and

F

destructive. Some people see it as an enjoyable, if cruel, sport. Avoid them. And if you're ever tempted to promise something you have no intention of delivering, think twice.

Forgiveness

Some crimes within a relationship are unforgivable; others can be forgiven with effort. But forgiveness has to be absolute. Asking you to forget is asking the impossible, but if you agree to forgive you cannot keep revisiting the crime and adding reproaches. As Marlene Dietrich said, 'A woman who forgives a man cannot keep reheating his sins for breakfast.' Forgiveness is not easy, but when it's done completely it can strengthen a relationship. Think carefully before you offer it, and make sure it's deserved before you commit to it. If you're not sure you're capable of it, Relate or Marriage Care will help you decide (see Help section).

Friends

You fall in love, and suddenly there seems to be only one thing in your life – being with your lover. You may have the occasional quiver of guilt, and vow to ring your friends asap,

F

but then he or she breathes on your cheek and ... whoops! ... friendship is forgotten. Hopefully you'll come to your senses after a while, and, if they're good friends, they'll forgive the gap in communication. If the bond between you wasn't strong, you may well lose them. A study by the Institute of Cognitive and Evolutionary Anthropology at Oxford University revealed that, on average, a new romance leads to the loss of two close friends, friends you could need if the big romance withers. Sometimes, and worryingly, a new partner can set out to isolate you from your friends because of his or her own insecurities. Blinded by love, you can miss what is happening and find yourself, later in life, turning to friends who no longer exist.

With almost one in two marriages ending in divorce, the need for friendship is greater than ever, but that need is a two-way thing. You can't hope to hold on to your friends while exiling your partner's. Yes, it's annoying if your woman is yakking to her friends on the phone for hours, or your man is sharing a few tinnies with the friends he shared tinnies with five minutes ago, or so it seems. Once upon a time, it was men who wanted to remain 'one of the lads' after marriage; now, women are doing it, too. And, when surveyed, women are less likely than men to name their partner as their best friend. But friends can never threaten a healthy relationship, so why fear them? If you're a woman, you tend to have control of the

F

social calendar, so play fair and make sure there's space for his friends as well as your own. There is a need for couples to have private time, without the intrusion of friends or family, but it doesn't need to be 24/7. True friends are there when you need them: make sure you keep them in your life. Each adult entering a relationship has history, and friends are part of that history. Hopefully, your partner's friends can be enjoyed; if not, they must be endured because they are an integral part of the person you love. Start to chip away at history, and you risk wounding not only your partner but your relationship itself. If the friends are yours, loyalty to them is laudable, but once you embark on a relationship you have to give weight to your partner's needs, too. Cherish friendships, but if you want your relationship to last, make sure they don't intrude into areas that are meant to be intimate. According to the Office for National Statistics, an average working couple with children spend only an hour and a quarter together in a day. Compare that with the time you spend with favourite colleagues. Hopefully, friends and lovers can co-exist. It's up to you to see that they do.

Sometimes a close friend will take up with someone you don't like. You may think them untrustworthy, or arrogant and rude, or out for all they can get. You may have the instinctive feeling that they mean trouble. You value your friend, and don't want to see them hurt. Nevertheless, unless you're asked your opinion it's better not to interfere. If your friend is deeply infatuated, he or she won't believe you, anyway, and you may lose a friend. Unless you have real proof of wrongdoing – two-timing or financial trickery – it's best to keep quiet, and make sure you're there if things go wrong. He or she will need your sympathy then.

Friends with benefits aka fuck-buddies

See Sex Without Strings

Dating your Best Friend's ex: They've been apart for ages, he or she has found someone else, you've always fancied him or her – so why shouldn't you make a move? And yet, at the back of your head, a little voice is saying, 'There'll be trouble.'

A lot depends on how they split up. If your friend was the one to say it was over, that makes it much easier. If he or she was dumped, however, you have to ask yourself whether history could repeat itself, with you getting the heave-ho this time. If the split was by mutual consent, and your friend is a reasonable person, there shouldn't really be any bar to your dating the ex. After all, an ex is not a scalp taken to be retained, hanging from your belt. If it does cause trouble, perhaps you need to look at your friendship and decide

F

whether it's worth it. You also have to decide how much this new relationship means to you. If it's just a whim, I'd let it go. If you feel it could become important to you, and there were no unsavoury aspects to the end of their relationship, then I think you should feel free to go ahead. Don't keep it secret from your friend, but don't rush to fill them in on details. And never, never compare notes.

F

SHE SAYS: If he's coming round for a meal, you have three options. Let him know the brutal truth: that kitchens are not your scene. Patronise the local deli, reasoning that your culinary ineptitude is best kept secret until you have become sexually indispensable. Or, third, remember the golden rule: meals for men need only contain meat and beer. (NB: Whichever course you take, remember never to serve gas-producing foods within two hours of bedtime.)

> *HE SAYS: The truth is, men are too straightforward to understand women, and the one man who figured it out died laughing before he could pass on the secret.*

SHE SAYS: They can remember the number of their first car, their PIN and the telephone number of Moss Bros suit hire. But the anniversary of the day you met? That's beyond their ken. Unless it happened to fall on Cup Final Day, in which case it's imprinted on their memory, and that makes things worse.

> *HE SAYS: She says a nice saloon would be best and you want to keep just a hint of Man About Town. Besides, you couldn't fold your legs into a Ford Focus and you won't contemplate amputation, not even for her.*

Friends with benefits aka fuck-buddies

HE SAYS: She's silent for five minutes. You ask what's up, and she says 'Nothing!' Search your conscience. Have you neglected to walk the dog, take out the trash, put up some shelves? If you've forgotten one of those things, you're in the doghouse. Two of them, and your clothes will be tossed out of the window and the locks changed.

> *SHE SAYS: Accept that men were born to poke the campfire, not to stir the pot. In time we can change that, but not overnight.*

HE SAYS: The way to a man's heart is no longer through his stomach. Nor, contrary to common belief, is it situated twelve inches below that organ. It lies in his ego, that tiny, intangible thing which governs his every move. Bruise it at your peril.

> *SHE SAYS: Once upon a time a man walked on the outside of the pavement so you didn't get splashed. Nowadays he sends you to get the car in case his hair gets wet. Chivalry is not only dead, it's cremated and the ashes scattered.*

HE SAYS: Men may be from Mars but women are from Broadmoor.

Game-playing

You hope that most people contemplating a relationship see it as a serious matter. Most people do. They may cause pain eventually, but they certainly won't inflict it for fun, or enjoy doing it. There are some people, however, who regard the whole thing as an opportunity to manipulate other people. They rejoice in creating tension, blowing hot and cold, saying maybe, teasing and tantalising, suddenly aloof then more loving than ever – all without any intention of ever bringing a relationship to fruition. Often, what they are doing is more visible to outsiders than to the victim. He or she lives on promises, and the hope that tomorrow things will get better. They believe elaborate plans when they're laid before them, and will prepare for that brilliant night out, that magic holiday that the game player has no intention of bringing about. Game-players share some traits with scalp-hunters,

G

except the fun for them is in tormenting, not simply collecting another victim. If you have any reason to think you are in the hands of game player, *get out quick* (*see also* Gold-diggers, Scalp-hunters and Love Rats).

Getting back

You parted, never to meet again – or so you said. Now you're having second thoughts. If it was a little spat, you can fly back mouthing 'Sorry,' and hope that all will be forgiven. If it was a bigger rift – if, for instance, one of you moved out and possessions were shared – it's not that easy. It's best to take a little while out before you make overtures. That gives you time to think over your feelings. Are you looking back with rose-coloured spectacles? If it was bad enough for you to leave in the first place, what has changed? Is it that you're simply missing him or her, and want to fill the gap?

If, after considering all these things, you still want to try again, don't suddenly appear on your ex's doorstep. If you do that, you risk a rebuff simply because you seem to be taking for granted the fact that you can walk back in. Better to write a letter suggesting that, after being together and being happy, there may be things to discuss. Unless you were 100 per cent in the wrong, don't apologise: all you're asking for is a meeting. If he or she turns down your overture, accept it. Don't rush to Facebook to tell the world that he or she has no heart. They may be thinking it over, and getting ready to make an overture of their own; and seeing you telling the world about what should be a private matter would make them think again. If, on the other hand, they seize your offer and suggest a meeting, have it on neutral ground and take it slowly. Relationships *can* be mended if there is good will on both sides. They can even be stronger for the mend. But the reasons for the original break-up need to be discussed if you want to prevent a recurrence. Next time there may be no going back.

Gifts

Don't be tempted to throw money at the problem of what to give a loved one, especially in the early stages of a relationship. If what you buy at huge expense is exactly what he or she wanted, they'll be thrilled, but then they'll feel they have to reciprocate, and an escalating *spendfest* will ensue. If, on the other hand, you spent a week's salary on the wrong thing, they'll think you're an idiot. Best to spend more effort than cash, in a ratio of 3 to 1, and find out exactly what would please them (see Buying Love).

G

Giving 100 per cent

Don't for a moment think I'm suggesting that you should work at a relationship 60 minutes of every hour, 24/7. A good relationship will have periods when both sides are busy elsewhere, or, even in another's company, getting on with their own thing. But all relationships, even those made in heaven, require some effort; and sometimes a change in the way we conduct our interpersonal relationships. 'I don't like rows, so I just walk away,' someone will say, quite proudly, as though ducking the issue were somehow noble. Another will spend a couple of hours chatting on Facebook, and then find it hard to drum up two words for his or her beloved. 'You know I can't say things like that,' is a poor excuse for not occasionally saying, 'I love you madly.'

Then again, there are hobbies. If your lover is football mad, you don't have to learn the offside rule, but you do need to take an intelligent interest in the progress of his or her team. A study for the dating site Forget Dinner found that conversation between married people dwindled over the years, when, considering their shared experiences, the amount they had to talk about should have increased. As in marriage, so it can be in relationships. If you'd rather watch a DVD or *Love Story* than chat with the him in your life, if you think giving her a bunch of garage flowers obviates the need to ask about her day, you'd better ask yourself what you're doing in the relationship. Are you staying because it's better than being alone?

Gold-diggers, love rats and scalp-hunters

Most people are in search of a good relationship, but some, mercifully not too many, are in that search for the wrong reasons. They may be after material or status gain, they may simply want one more scalp to hang on their belt, or, especially on the internet, they may be playing some twisted game. Male or female, they may be rats, scuttling around the emotional highways causing misery. It's important not to make snap judgements about another's motives, but if you have reason to believe you may be getting entangled with someone who will exploit your emotions, or pick your pocket, you have really only one alternative: get out quick (*see also* Game-Playing).

Guilt

Unless it's channelled into action, guilt is a useless emotion. Don't mistake it for remorse, which is true repentance and means you realise you've done wrong and won't do it again.

G

Guilt is that thing that gnaws away at you, turning you into a nervous wreck or someone who is always begging forgiveness, when what they really want is someone to take the burden of guilt away from them. Used properly, however, guilt can be productive. Weigh up your crime, and then work out what you can do to make reparation. Simply owning up is not enough, particularly if, by telling, you make someone else unhappy. If you stole, can you repay, if not to the victim then to a charity? If you caused pain, can you relieve pain, there or elsewhere? If you caused someone to misjudge someone else, can you take back your words? If all else fails, do a penance: work for a charity or do favours for those who need them, until you think your debt is repaid. Once you've done that, lay your guilt aside and move on.

Guilty secrets

We all have a past. When we enter into a relationship we have to make decisions about how much of that past is ours to keep secret, and how much we are willing to share. It's best to be honest about anything that is known to other people, for instance a criminal conviction; but you only need to be this honest when the relationship is moving towards permanency (see Dartboard). A termination of pregnancy, something you

G

did not confide to others, is yours to keep to yourself, unless it would have any bearing on your future child-bearing. The secrets of members of your family or circle of friends, which should have little or no bearing on your future together, are not matters that you should feel the need to confide. The yardstick when deciding what or what not to tell should be two-fold: does it threaten your future together; and how would you feel if you discovered that he/she had kept the same thing from you? (*See also* Sexual History.)

HE SAYS: Men can pee standing up, have more control of their lachrymal glands, and get fewer headaches than women. On the other hand, we are constitutionally incapable of caring for plants, and go completely to pieces if abandoned in lingerie departments, because we don't know where to put our eyes.

> *SHE SAYS: He knows Valentine's Day is coming for 364 days, but still scribbles a heart on a used envelope and tells you the card shop was shut.*

HE SAYS: Asking for a date outright used to work in your father's day, but progress and the courts have rendered it obsolete. Your father met your mother when his Auntie Millie asked her to tea, but that was the Golden Age, when life was straightforward. Now we live in Politically Correct times, which is French for 'Bloody Awkward'.

> *SHE SAYS: To be born a man is to be born to privilege. To be born a woman is still a stumbling block – something to be surmounted.*

HE SAYS: She wants your body all right, but sometimes it seems as though she'd like it hanging from a tree.

Habits

In the first flush of love, the object of our affections has no bad habits. As time goes on, this can change. That delightful little quirk becomes an obsession, in your eyes. It can make you feel murderous. Ask yourself if it really matters. If it doesn't, learn to ignore it. If it does matter, speak out. If you do, however, be prepared to hear that you are not immune to bad habits yourself.

Before you speak out you need to be very sure that a habit is a bad habit. The fact that it annoys you is not proof: someone else might be able to co-exist happily with it. And if it's not a bad habit, or if your loved one refuses to change it, then you have to decide whether or not you can live with it (*see also* Vices).

H

Hang-ups

We all have hang-ups. Yes, I know you're the exception, but read on anyway. A hang-up is a minor obsession that can be irritating or worrying. It can stem from insecurity, in which case the right relationship could cure it, or it can come from nowhere. If you're really in love, you can live with the adored one's single hang-up – at a pinch, with two. If they have more hang-ups than the average wardrobe, you need to think it through carefully.

Harassment

The Protection from Harassment Act 1997 says: 'A person must not pursue a course of conduct which amounts to harassment of another, and which he knows or ought to know amounts to harassment of the other. For the purposes of this section, the person whose course of conduct is in question ought to know that it amounts to harassment of another if a reasonable person in possession of the same information would think the course of conduct amounted to harassment of the other.' In other words, if you're making someone's life a misery with calls, letters, texts, face-to-face confrontations, or anything else unwelcome, you may be committing an offence,

H

particularly if any kind of threat is involved. If you feel you may be being subjected to harassment, keep a written record of what happens, and if it shows no signs of diminishing talk to the police.

Holidays

For some couples, a holiday is an oasis of pleasure, a chance to get to know one another without all the pressures of workaday life. But being together 24/7 can also expose any flaws in the relationship. For ten days or two weeks you pretend to be living together. You see one another in the morning, at the end of a long day, a little the worse for alcohol, or suddenly exposed to the attention of strangers. Don't have huge expectations of a holiday. You may have two weeks of enchantment; or you may not. A holiday can make or break a relationship, so be prepared for the after-effects. If two weeks together convinces you that a lifetime together would be hell on earth, part as friends and move on. If, on the other hand, two weeks together whetted your appetite for more, think yourself lucky. Unpack your cases and get on with your life.

H

Holiday romance

Can you meet the man/woman of your dreams on holiday? Yes, you can. Thousands of people have. But the holiday atmosphere can have a heady effect. That Orlando Bloom look-alike you met in the Algarve may look distinctly un-starry back in Walton-on-Thames. Sun, sand, and sangria can also lead to a lot of promises that may not be easy to keep when you return to reality. So, pack only reasonable expectations along with your scuba gear, and don't let yourself get carried away until you're back home and the promises have borne fruit.

H

SHE SAYS: This guy has hands that cover more territory than Christopher Columbus. When he finds out your reflexes are better than his, he tells you he has to fill in next year's tax demand – and it's only July. Up until then you were rehearsing seven ways of making sure you never saw him again. So why must you quell the desire to run after him and demand a second chance?

> *HE SAYS: Women stick together. Your sister, who has a Judas streak a yard wide, fills her in on your shortcomings. The Time You Stole the Last Kit Kat (which should have been hers), The Time You Forgot to Feed the White Mice (and they ate their tails), and finally The Time You Took a Girl Out in Your Father's Car (and it rolled into a ditch while you were snogging).*

SHE SAYS: Driving you to his place or yours does not count as foreplay.

> *HE SAYS: 'How do you feel?' she'll say. You say 'OK,' and she says, 'No, how do you really feel?' or even worse, 'What do you feel like doing?' Tell the truth – that you feel like watching telly – and she will recoil. You'll get a lecture on insensitivity, and have to rush to the all-night garage for flowers.*

Holiday romance

HE SAYS: Women are not only as smart as men, they are every bit as ruthless. To suggest they're not is to perpetuate the 'weaker sex' image that held women back for centuries. Today her claws may be French-manicured, but they can still scratch.

> *SHE SAYS: There's a statistic that says a high percentage of relationships originate in the workplace. That may be true, but work is where you go to achieve rapid promotion and oodles of cash. You dreamed about it at university: it's called getting on. It's a pity that the man of your dreams doesn't want you to be the youngest executive in the building. He wants you to look like Scarlett Johansson.*

HE SAYS: Put women in the passenger seat and they come into their own. Probably the first words Eve said to Adam were, 'You're too close to the snake in front.'

> *SHE SAYS: 'I'll call you' is a get-out half the time – and who cares? Like buses, there'll be another along any minute.*

HE SAYS: Ever since Juliet wittered on about wherefore Romeo was, some woman somewhere has been looking for the man who got away.

I

Identity

The man or woman you attract was drawn to you because of what you are: your personality, your likes and dislikes, your place in the world. Becoming part of a twosome doesn't mean you have to surrender that identity. Nor do you have to be together 24/7. Separate pastimes are OK where there is trust. No need to suffer at football games, or pretend to understand the offside rule – he didn't choose you because you reminded him of Wayne Rooney. And if she likes chamber music, there's no reason you should work for a Ph.D. on Bach.

Be there for your partner when they come home from the match or the concert. Show an interest in what they have to tell you about their evening. That's more than enough.

I

If not the one, *then anyone*

As you get older, particularly if your biological clock starts ticking (and that happens to men too), you can start to feel needy. You want someone's arms around you, or someone in your arms. That's when it can be tempting to settle for someone 'nice'. You compromise. You pretend. You try to convince yourself it's the real thing; and the look of relief on your mother's face reinforces that idea. Don't just settle for someone: that isn't fair on you, and it certainly isn't fair on the other man or woman. Don't let anything panic you into a relationship. The day after you've tied the knot could be the very day *the one* arrives in your life.

Independence (and dependence)

If I had to name one quality that almost guarantees a good relationship, it's mutual respect for the other's individuality. That means that you respect your lover's right to make their own decisions in every area of life, which is independence. However, there's another side to independence within a relationship. Just as you appreciate your right to make your own decisions, you must respect your partner's right to do the same. That can lead to difficulties sometimes, but, with discussion and where love and respect exist, these can be worked through.

If your independence is detracting from your partner's quality of life, you need to consider whether or not you are being too demanding. If your partner seeks to cut back your independence, don't be afraid to speak up, but not before you have fully considered whether or not there is merit in what they say.

Dependence is the opposite of independence, and is not a state most of us are happy with. However, many good and lasting relationships have been based on one partner's being completely dependent on the other, so it can work where there is good will. But just as you must weigh up your right to independence, you must also carefully consider whether being dependent, or expecting your partner to be dependent on you, is strictly fair. Relationships can go wrong, partners can die, and the dependent one will find themselves suddenly cast adrift. In a good and loving relationship, both partners are dependent on one another to a certain extent, but careful thought is necessary with regard to degree.

I

Infidelity

In this sexually liberated age, it may surprise you to know that the latest British Social Attitudes Survey claims that 91 per cent of women aged 18 to 24 think that infidelity is wrong. Women over 60 are more tolerant, at only 83 per cent. Twice as many men as women confessed to having been unfaithful, but the figures were small: 17 per cent against 8 per cent. In spite of this disapproval, though, infidelity is on the increase. Half of all respondents in another survey agreed that they knew someone who was having an affair. Today you will find people who tell you that a little bit of straying spices up a relationship. Many of the 200 American women surveyed admitted to infidelity, and claimed that, as long as it was undiscovered, it did spice things up. Now there are even agencies to help you stray, and one of them claims to have 600,000 members.

My own opinion is that, in seven out of ten cases, infidelity is the ruin of a relationship. It may survive the initial discovery, but trust will have been replaced by mistrust, and sooner or later that leads to ruin. The couples who manage to survive infidelity will probably have an even stronger relationship, but a lot of tears will have been shed before that happy state is reached. The latest craze is 'Intelligent Adultery': it originated in America, and put simply it means 'Don't get caught.' If nobody knows, nobody gets hurt – that's the theory. The trouble is that 'intelligent' is not the word to apply to adultery. You're almost bound to get caught, and when you do you're in trouble.

Sometimes, and often in work situations, a man or woman will meet someone with whom attraction is so strong it sweeps away every other consideration. I call these 'great loves', and trying to resist them is like trying to hold back the sea. But 'great loves' are scarcer than hen's teeth. More often there's an initial attraction that makes you stray, but won't last. Losing a good relationship for a flash-in-the-pan affair doesn't make sense. So, if it's just a strong attraction, walk away. If you think it may be a 'great love', ask Relate to help you sort out whether or not it's as good as it seems.

Infidelity needn't mean the end of a relationship. Many men and women who have entered into affairs or one-night stands never, for a second, stopped loving their partner. But a lot depends on degree. A drunken snog at the office party is very different from the discovery that there has been another man or woman for years. Sometimes infidelity can serve as a wake-up call to a relationship. If the 'wronged' partner is wise enough to examine their own behaviour as well as their partner's, it may emerge that more attention to one another's needs is all that is necessary. What doesn't work is to shrug the shoulders and adopt a 'put up and shut up' attitude. Whatever material benefits exist within a relationship, if infidelity isn't properly dealt with, bitterness will grow. If you were secretly tired of the sexual side of your relationship, and are happy to see your partner satisfied elsewhere, think seriously about whether or not you're in the right place. And if sex with your partner has become a little dull, why not mimic an affair: book into an hotel for a night, have a romantic dinner as though with a stranger, and be adventurous in bed. To keep it authentic, the man should exit in the small hours, carrying his shoes. (Only joking.) (*See also* Trust.)

In-laws

Like them or loathe them, there's no escaping them. Once you accept that, however much you might wish it, they will not disappear, you can set about seeing what must be endured, what can be enjoyed, and what can be changed.

Affection compensates for much within your own family; in-laws do not come with that degree of familiarity. Make allowances for differences in upbringing, and try to understand their code, even if you will never make it your own. Remember that they have invested decades of love and care in your partner, so you can't expect them simply to turn him or her over to you and retreat to the back row. Involve them in special days, make sure they have some time alone with your partner, and can get access to them whenever they choose. If your partner is a bit forgetful, jog his or her memory about special days or achievements.

When you have done your best to accommodate them, if there are still rough patches, allow things to flow over you. They matter, but not as much as the nuclear family, which is you and your lover.

Is it worth it?

You're hanging in there at work, or in a relationship, and it's hell. You wake in the morning trying to tell yourself today will be better, and knowing in your heart that it won't. After all, bad as things are, might not the alternative be worse? So you strain every sinew, watch your words, and try to keep a smile on your partner's face, all the while waiting for the next inevitable explosion.

Ask yourself: is it worth it? And if, on consideration, you decide it isn't, be brave enough to make a change (*see also* Worth It).

I

Issues

Sometimes, in an otherwise good relationship, issues will arise with your partner. Perhaps alcohol, or gambling, even drugs. Or it may be something relatively simple, like being animal-mad, or fussy over food. How you react will depend on the seriousness of the issue. For instance, drug addiction is not something that can be settled by a quiet talk. Your reaction will also be governed by how deeply you care, and how long the relationship has been in existence. Unless it's something relatively simple, it's best to get help. Your GP can be one source, and many others are listed in the Help section at the back of this book.

I

HE SAYS: Men believe they'll go on holiday and meet a blonde with a Ph.D. and a private income. Oh, they know all the pitfalls – how you can opt for a horny weekend, and by the end of it she's entitled to half your pension. Or you swop phone numbers and find out her ex is a psychopath who can't tolerate anyone sleeping in his footsteps. And still they Google 'Single breaks'.

> *SHE SAYS: One day she'll want a man and kids, but not yet. Her mother keeps talking about stability, but she already has it: a salary cheque.*

HE SAYS: That's the thing about male friendship. Blokes don't witter on about best friends, and one for all, and all that guff. They live it. They do grown-up stuff. Women cling on to each other, and giggle, and whisper, and tell one another every bleeding thing. Men aren't like that.

> *SHE SAYS: Men are pack animals, and when in packs they run amok. Even singly they can make you cringe, clicking their fingers for service, talking to your cleavage; they even do that in the office, mistaking your knee for dough that wants kneading.*

SHE SAYS: 'I've got my reasons,' means 'I shouldn't have done it, but what's it got to do with you?' 'What did I do this time?' is the old attack-as-the-best-means-of-defence ploy. 'I'll fix it later,' is tricky because it has two interpretations: 'If I leave it, you might do it,' and 'I don't know how to do it and don't want you to know.' Either way, it's quicker (and probably cheaper) to get a tradesman. 'I don't want to see you again,' comes out as 'You're too good for me,' or 'I don't want to tie you down.' And the worst of it is, they think we believe it.

> HE SAYS: Once a man has a woman officially, he seems to go off the boil. She becomes 'The Missus' or 'The Wife'. Once he couldn't get away quickly enough to meet her; now he takes to going to the pub after work, and switching off his mobile when she rings.

SHE SAYS: Men cannot multi-task. He can pee, or he can manage the seat, but not both together.

> HE SAYS: There's a finality about the word 'Commitment' which can be chilling. You may love the woman, but you also love your car – you're even passionate about it, but the next year there's a new model. It's a sobering thought, isn't it? A motor you can trade in. A wife's for life.

Jealousy

There are a few, a very few, people who have a jealous nature. Most people who exhibit the signs of jealousy are actually motivated by fear, by the feeling that everyone else has more right to exist, more to offer than you have. When you want to rubbish that girl your partner smiled at, it's not jealousy: it's fear that he will prefer her, because she's so much better than you. That's what happens when someone can't stand their mother or father-in-law. 'He/she is bound to care more for him/her, because I'm not worth caring about,' is what they are really saying to themselves.

Jealousy can be especially strong with regard to siblings, as you convince yourself that they are more loved than you. Alternatively, you begrudge anyone who has time with your

J

beloved, for the simple reason that you think he'll enjoy it more than the time spent with you. At its worst, jealousy can make you hate anyone who achieves happiness – why should they have what you fear you never will get? If you're not careful, jealousy can become almost a full-time job. You try to cut your partner off from contact with anyone who might steal away his or her affections.

In doing so, you make yourself unattractive, and make the chance of their straying that much greater, because jealousy is a deeply unattractive quality. Turn to Self-esteem and start to really value yourself for who you are; then jealousy will become a thing of the past.

J

HE SAYS: Fat is the bear in the woods as far as women are concerned. Say something harmless like 'You're OK as you are,' and all hell breaks loose. Believe it or not, that simple remark is seen as an insult. In womanspeak it means, 'You're a mess, but there's nothing to be done about it.' And don't say, 'That dress makes you look slim.' This will be construed as, 'You're fat, but that dress makes you look marginally less fat.'

> *SHE SAYS: Getting your own place is better than sex – at least at first. When you realise you've been seeing one guy regularly, it shakes you. So much so that you panic, and write him a Dear John. But you add a smiley at the end just in case you change your mind.*

HE SAYS: You say, quite nicely, 'Can I have some bread with this corned beef?' and back comes, 'Please yourself.' When you realise she's not getting up for it, you go yourself, but the bread bin's empty and she knew that. You'll be sleeping back-to-back tonight, and she'll give a little sob every time she senses you're dropping off.

> *SHE SAYS: The male sigh can trigger sprinklers on three floors of Selfridge's and all because you can't immediately choose between aqua and turquoise.*

Jealousy 123

HE SAYS: Nowadays, not only must you not touch, you mustn't comment on appearance. 'That's a nice sweater,' will get you a glare. A term of endearment, or an offer to help with a heavy object, is taboo. You will be termed 'patronising' or 'disgusting', and either ostracised or reported, depending on whom you offended. Even the sensible ones are scared of letting down their side. There are times when you can envisage the human race dying out altogether, because no one will make the first move any more.

> *SHE SAYS: Stories abound of women who slept their way to the boardroom, but you don't believe them, largely because women at the top never have messed-up lipstick, much less a post-coital flush. No, if women make it as far as the glass ceiling you can be sure they earned it. One of these days a woman will bust right through it (OK, so you know about Marjorie Scardino but as a general rule . . .) and then it will be a fairer world.*

HE SAYS: Genius is one per cent inspiration and 99 per cent some other bugger's effort.

> *SHE SAYS: You make a few simple rules – put towels on rails, put lids back on jars – and the next minute he's goose-stepping round the kitchen, forefinger under his nostrils, shouting 'Achtung!*

K

Keen aka desperation

OK, he or she is the best thing to come your way in a long time. You want to shower them with attention, occupy their every waking moment, be at their beck and call. You call it being keen. He or she may see it as desperation, an unattractive quality. So, at first at least, play it cool. That way it can only get better, and if it goes wrong at least you've kept your dignity.

There's a danger in being too keen – or even desperate. It can lead you to convince yourself that at last you've found *the one*. You need to justify your own desperation, and this can lead to terrible mistakes. Play it cool, for your own sake.

K

Keep it to yourself

In the early days of a relationship, it's best not to talk too much about it. I don't mean keep it secret, but putting every little detail of a first date on Facebook is a big mistake. How would you feel if you saw your every word and action being passed around total strangers, and commented on into the bargain? Or heard from a friend of a friend that a blow-by-blow description has been given by phone? If the affair progresses, you can gradually be more open. If it fizzles out, as many do, you won't have to give explanations. I know it's fun to share the news that you had a brilliant night out, and there's no harm in that. But spare the detail, at least at first.

Kiss and make up

Nothing sweeter than making up. You're hurt and angry, and so is your partner, and then suddenly you're in one another's arms. Heaven! But unless it was just a silly spat and best forgotten, don't let the bliss of kiss-and-make-up rule out the need to discuss why you rowed in the first place. And if you feel that kissing and making up is 'giving way', then making the first move to reconciliation and getting down off your high horse is a sign of strength, not weakness.

K

SHE SAYS: Men can be divided into three categories: Bachelors, Husbands and Drivers. There's something about a long, shiny bonnet that twangs a man's cerebral cortex. Men have five different Y chromosomes, each paired to its own X. This makes them susceptible to the smell of petrol.

> *HE SAYS: On the average, a man gets seven erections a day but most of them are in his sleep; and she's just wasted one of the waking ones sending you downstairs to check the gas.*

SHE SAYS: One day, you tell yourself, he will arrive, and he will be a SUD: Single, Upwardly mobile and Drop-dead gorgeous. Until that day comes, you refuse to join in the gossip, or the pursuit of any even remotely eligible man. You're saving yourself for him.

> *HE SAYS: Women can cry more easily than men because their bladder is situated nearer their eyes. They can turn the tears on and off at will and produce little heaving noises in their chest. And against your will it turns you on and that's exactly what they intended. You've said 'Sorry' although you still don't know what you've done.*

Kiss and make up

HE SAYS: God created Adam, and gave him Eden. Then he created Eve, in case Adam, was enjoying himself.

> *SHE SAYS: You know the feeling – you're good at your job, and you pay your tab. You're a Modern Woman. On your 25th birthday, however, your mother is liable to ring tearfully to say she hopes to live to see her grandchildren. As she's only 45, you can bear this reproach with equanimity: 'One day, Mother, one day.' For now, there's other fish to fry.*

HE SAYS: Humdrum, that's what commitment is. The end of adventure, the death of opportunity. Sod's law means that the day after the wedding, the very day, you'll find the woman of your dreams at the next desk, across the aisle in a plane. And it will be too late.

> *SHE SAYS: Friends mutter darkly about playing around, and your mother may send you a framed, embroidered version of the old rhyme, 'Too many rings around Rosie, Rosie gets no ring at all.' When this elicits no response, she might start phoning weekly with tales of cousins' betrothals, and women who discovered too late that they were infertile. She tells anyone who will listen that all her daughter cares about is her career.*

Laughter

Dr David Delvin, a famous sex-doctor, once said that a laugh was worth a thousand orgasms. Laughter can banish the blues, heal wounds, diffuse rows, and generally make the world a better place. It doesn't have to be a belly-laugh, a quiet chuckle will do. As long as there are plenty of them.

Letters

If you fear a face-to-face meeting for some reason, a letter can sometimes work wonders. Write it, and put it aside for at least 12 hours. Read it, and rewrite as necessary until you feel comfortable with it. Letters can also help if there has been a long absence, perhaps because of a row. What have you got to lose if you send a conciliatory letter? You might regain a

L

friend – even a lover. I don't approve of Dear John letters: if someone was worth having a relationship with, surely they deserve a face-to-face goodbye, or at least some suggestion that all is not well? If you must write one, try putting yourself in your soon-to-be-ex-lover's place. It's no good telling them how wonderful they are but you're dumping them anyway. However, you should do all you can to prevent them from feeling diminished. Don't, whatever you do, use the hoary old 'You're too good for me' line. It really is the pits. You must write your own letter, but here's a rough idea of where to go:

Dear John,

I have so much enjoyed the last six months. We shared so much that was pleasurable and stimulating, and will stay in my memory. However, in the last few weeks I have felt, as I'm sure you have felt too, that we had differences in our outlook and aims which would be hard to reconcile if we stayed together. You have the capacity to make someone wonderfully happy, and I know you will go on to have a deep and lasting relationship. I can only hope I will be as lucky. I hope, too, that eventually we can be the friends we were when we first met. If you wish otherwise I will understand. Thank you for some wonderful memories,

X

Libido

Loss of libido, the desire to make love, is distressing. It can also be destructive of a relationship, if the other partner mistakes that lack of desire for rejection. The desire to bolster the flagging male libido has turned Viagra into a billion-pound industry (the NHS spends £58 million a year on the drug), so it's no surprise that pharmaceutical companies are racing to find the female equivalent.

One survey claimed that 43 per cent of women suffer from Female Sexual Dysfunction, compared with just 30 per cent of men who have erectile dysfunction. There are several sub-divisions: what used to be called low sex drive is now 'hypoactive sexual desire disorder'; inability to get turned on is 'female sexual arousal disorder'; not reaching a climax with your partner is 'anorgasmia'; inability to relax is 'sexual pain disorder'. Don't let these titles scare you. Chances are your low libido has a simple, easily correctible cause. The desire may still be there, in both men and women – it's simply that the body won't oblige. This may be due to illness, depression, or medication. Stress, tiredness, lack of self-esteem, or guilt can all play their part, and a natural loss of desire may follow childbirth, although this usually disappears in time. Post-menopausal women can experience a fall in libido, but this responds well to treatment.

L

If, after gentle wooing and encouragement, the condition persists, it needs expert help to define the cause and put things right, so the first stop should be your GP. Don't be embarrassed. Doctors are human beings, and liable to suffer all the conditions that afflict the rest of us. If not, they'll certainly have heard the story thousands of times before. If temporary loss of libido has followed childbirth, talk to your Health Visitor about it, and if it persists, seek help from your GP. But don't despair: treatments exist, and there are currently more than 20 potential cures in development, ranging from nasal sprays to skin patches, some based on hormonal treatment. At least one is available in patch form on the NHS, for post-menopausal women. It will be a pity if these treatments become lifestyle drugs used by women with no sexual problems who simply want to increase their libido, as happened with Viagra – about 60 per cent of the men who use it are believed to have no erectile problems. Around 900,000 men in Britain are said to have used it at least once.

Problems can arise when two people in an otherwise happy relationship have different levels of desire. Compromise is the answer here, and, if compromise proves difficult, turn to Relate or Marriage Care (see Help section; *see also* Sex).

Licking your wounds

Your lover has gone, you're all alone, and it feels like the end of the world. We've all been there. Going over the same old ground is useless, as you never come to a conclusion. And this is where your memory starts to play tricks: it works selectively. You don't remember the rows, or the cheating, or the way she tried to put you down: you remember her, fragrant and affectionate after a shower. You don't remember the time he stayed out all night: you remember the one time he brought you breakfast in bed, or pushed a bunch of gorgeous flowers round the door to say sorry. This selection is to be resisted. Make a list of all that was good in the relationship and then a list – a true list – of what wasn't. If the good outweighs the bad, write him a letter, but don't post it. Put it in a drawer for consideration tomorrow. Pamper yourself a little, and make sure you eat healthily. We've all seen the photographs of celebrities, drawn and unattractive after break-up. It isn't a pretty look and it's one you don't want.

If you're licking your wounds after break-up, it's important to have a breathing space to understand yourself, analyse what went wrong, and think what you're looking for in a subsequent relationship. (If you've never had a relationship, but want to find one, this can help, too.) You need to feel relaxed and happy in your own company before you

L

enter into any relationship. You need answers to questions such as what you want from your relationship and what else you want from life. Up to now, you will have been learning from your parents' relationship, from your relationship with siblings, friends, and from any relationships you've had, good or bad. Think about what has affected you most, what you'd like to copy in a new relationship, and what you'd prefer to avoid. Once break-up is behind you, will you be happy and balanced, or do you feel needy or desperate? How comfortable do you feel about socialising? Do you really want another relationship, or are you just afraid of being alone? Are you happy with your own behaviour in the past, with parents, siblings, friends, or partners? If not, now is the time to change. Don't think about what you want in a partner, think also about what you have to give, and whether or not it's enough.

The most attractive people are those who are happy within themselves, which is different from being self-satisfied or arrogant, two most unattractive traits. Do you tell yourself, 'I'll be happy when I'm thin,' or 'I need to be more outgoing'? Do you feel you have to make an effort, just to justify your existence? If so, see Self-esteem. When you feel up to it, write a list of the things you want to do in the next two weeks. Include plenty of socialising. Now is a time for giving yourself a good time (*see also* In the Zone; and if you want to talk things through, see the Help section).

Lies

We all lie at times – white lies, little lies, because it's easier than a long explanation. But when lies become an everyday occurrence, they're a sign that something is wrong. Compulsive lying is an illness that requires help. It can cause distress both to the liar and the deceived, but it is not a crime: it is a symptom of underlying trauma, which needs expert attention. If you or your partner find the need to lie increasing, see the Help section.

However, there are some people who lie consistently from choice, and without compulsion, frequently in the hope of gain. They are dangerous, and can cause huge complications for anyone who becomes involved with them. If you have reason to believe you have become involved with a fraudulent liar, seek legal advice or go to the police.

Listening

One of the most attractive qualities in a man or woman is the capacity to listen. We all listen sometimes, but some of us do it in a half-hearted way, obviously longing for our turn to talk. Sometimes the listener is obviously thinking about something else, planning next day at the office or when to get their hair

L

cut. But the person who will give you their undivided attention immediately improves, not only your morale, but their chances of being someone you want to see again.

Loneliness

If you have recently come out of a relationship, there is a hole in your life, a hole that exists even if the relationship was latterly unhappy. If you've never had a relationship, you may still yearn for that special someone who will be there for you, backing you up, confiding in and listening to you. Without them, you're lonely, even though your day may be filled with colleagues, family, and friends. That kind of loneliness can be misleading: it can convince you that someone, anyone, is suitable to fill the hole in your life. By the time you've realised that he/she isn't right, you've both been hurt.

That's why you have to learn to deal with loneliness, to make it bearable and allow time for the right relationship to come along. The one thing that's sure is that love never climbed in your window: unless you're out there, mixing, it won't find you. So make sure you socialise. Join clubs, do voluntary work. Make friends of both sexes, because each friend you make has a network of friends and family. The one you seek could be lurking there.

Long distance

Can relationships survive separation? The answer, if they're strong, is 'Yes'. Nowadays, when both partners are likely to have careers, separation can be a real hazard. Sometimes one partner or another may be off to university, to a military posting, or to another part of the country in search of work. There are two things to be considered: communication and trust.

Nowadays, communication is easy – phone, Skype, email, social networks . . . take your pick. If the separation is prolonged, keep a diary so that your partner can see how your day goes. Keeping emotional intimacy is important: that text 'Love you' can mean a lot to someone on the other side of the country or the world.

Trust is more difficult. It's awfully easy to imagine your partner being tempted by someone else for no other reason than that you're not there. In fact, if there is love and commitment, it's easy to resist temptation. So curb your imagination, look forward to the homecoming, and remember that infidelity can occur on your doorstep. Distance doesn't make it more likely.

L

Loss

In Breaking Up, we have dealt with the traumatic effects of a relationship ending. In a sense, it's a bereavement. Sometimes, sadly, bereavement is all too real. Much of the advice in Breaking Up applies to the pain of bereavement, but it can really help to have some grief counselling (see Help section). Time does heal, but you are unlikely to believe that in the aftermath of loss; and talking with someone who not only sympathises but can guide you through that wasteland of sorrow is invaluable.

Love

Poets have written sonnets about it, great painters have immortalised it on canvas, but perhaps the Beatles summed it up best when they wrote 'All you need is love'. If you have it, you can survive any crisis, forgive any wrong. Give thanks for it every day. Very occasionally it comes at first sight; occasionally it sneaks up on you, and you find it in the last place you would have expected it. Most often it grows steadily until the person you quite liked becomes the person you can't live without. The thing that sets love apart is its staying power. It can't be bought, nor is it universally available, so if you're lucky enough to have it, hold on to it.

L

HE SAYS: Time of the Month is the elephant in the room. Pre-commitment you just avoid them when they go full-moon. Married, you have to live with PMT. You're stuck with it. (You're stuck all the time, come to that.) No prospect of getting trapped in a lift with Sarah Michelle Geller. You'll be round at your brother-in- law's helping paper the kitchen.

> *SHE SAYS: You ask 'Been out today?' 'Yes.'*
> *'Somewhere nice?' 'No.'*
> *This is known as the Wimbledon Technique. You serve, they bat back.*
> *'Did the weather hold up?' 'Depends what you mean by "hold-up".'*
> *Love-thirty to them.*

HE SAYS: He comes back from a hot date and the most he'll say is 'It was OK' Next month you'll be at Moss Bros getting kitted out because her mother wants the wedding in the Leatherhead Gazette but there's no need to chew it over now: not when Lineker's on the box.

> *SHE SAYS: Men have a mania for barbecues and feed you raw meat in a charred coating that smells of smoke. For the next four hours you keep checking your watch to see what time the salmonella will strike.*

SHE SAYS: *A man you've known for years catches you feeling low. You've always managed to avoid him, but now you say yes because it's better than nothing. He takes you to a nice restaurant, but you order the cheapest thing on the menu because you don't want to be beholden. The look in his eyes when you tell him every night is hair-wash night will haunt you for weeks.*

> HE SAYS: *I don't understand attraction. Does the guy who you'd think was plankton if you saw him swimming have some secret, mysterious knowledge? If not, how come he knows how to make a woman drool?*

SHE SAYS: *'I'll come in for coffee, but it's only fair to warn you I'll never love again,' is a non-starter.*

> HE SAYS: *Ever since Juliet wittered on about wherefore Romeo was, some woman somewhere has been looking for the man who got away.*

SHE SAYS: *You decide the cure for unrequited love is the two-pronged approach. This involves dating everything with a pulse while making detailed plans for snaring the real object of your affections. Set dates: Easter to get a night out with him, midsummer to get him into bed, Christmas the engagement, and pregnant by Twelfth Night.*

Making contact

We all know the scenario. You're on a train or in a queue, and you see someone who makes you catch your breath. The next day you see them again. It's fate, you think, but how do you make contact? For all the other person knows, you could be a psychopath. Try to identify their response. Are they aware of your interest? Are they looking around for the Transport Police? If it's a she, take into account that she's been warned from birth to be wary of strangers. If the object of your affections is male, remember it's still a bit *infra dig* for the woman to make the first move. On the other hand, you may never get another chance. Be brave and be prepared. If you haven't got a card, write down your phone number and email address. Hand it to him or her and say, 'If you'd care for a drink some time, this is how you contact me.' Then walk away. You may never hear from them. On the other hand . . .

M

Meeting

See also Dating

There are numerous ways to meet new people. The internet is increasingly popular. Lonely hearts columns abound. There are singles clubs and holidays, dating agencies, and speed-dating events. By far the most useful meetings, however, will be through friends, or work, or at some society or further-education class. And dance classes are becoming one of the best ways of meeting new people without strain (see Dance Classes. You'll find a comprehensive list of classes on the internet).

Millions of people world-wide are finding love on-line and some sites (see the Help section) employ psychologists, even anthropologists, to perfect their matchmaking. On some sites you will be asked to fill in a questionnaire giving your personal details, and covering matters such as whether or not you want children, whether income is important, and listing what you desire in a partner. Those running the site then trawl through all the variables, such as religion, politics, and ethnicity, add in your requirements, and – heigh ho – they come up with a list of possibles. One site, which targets the over-30s, makes members take a psychometric test of 250 questions. It then guides them through the first stages of a contact with suggested questions and answers. The advantage of internet dating is that

M

it gives you access to a huge pool of potential partners. The downside is that lying is easy on the world-wide web. Men tend to lie about their height, women about their weight or their age. Both sexes are inclined to suggest they earn more than they do, increasing their income by around 20 per cent.

Even if you have contacted someone through a reputable, recognised agency, it is essential to take precautions when first meeting. Make sure you meet in a well-populated place, introduce the person to a friend, and don't plan out-of-the way meetings until you know enough about them to feel safe. A sensible person will appreciate your caution – if they object, they're best avoided. The same caution should apply to anyone you meet through a message-board or lonely hearts ad.

Singles clubs are a good place to make friends, and so are further-education courses, drama societies and reading clubs. Their big advantage is that you're free of the embarrassment that can occur when a man and a woman meet in the hope of being attracted to one another. Your local library should have details of these. Most holiday agencies have details of singles holidays and weekends.

As I've mentioned, the one certain fact is that love never climbed in at your window, so get out there and mingle. Friends of either sex or any age have their own network of family and acquaintances. Once you have access to that network, you never know whom you might meet.

M

Mischief

You're secure in your relationship; in fact, you couldn't be happier. And then some kind friend, ever so innocently, tells you that your lover has been canoodling with someone else. 'I'm sure it was just a bit of fun,' they say in a tone that implies full penetrative sex. Or perhaps you see something on a social networking site; or there's that dodgy phone call that your partner can't explain. The bottom falls out of your world in five seconds flat.

So what should you do? First of all, establish the facts. Don't make accusations on flimsy evidence; and, however good the friend, their account is flimsy because they could have misconstrued what they saw, or, occasionally, be deliberately exaggerating for reasons of their own. Similarly, everything that comes up on the internet should carry a health warning. People can, and do, falsify entries there. Phone calls can be made by mischief-makers; and I've come across more than one case where an individual who lusted after someone who was already in a relationship deliberately created the illusion of an affair to cause tension between the partners.

So don't dive straight in. Above all, don't ring your mother (or anyone else) and express outrage. At this moment, this is between you and one other. Pick your time, and then say what you've been told or seen. Try not to sound accusing, and listen

M

to explanations. If your tone doesn't suggest that the sky is about to fall, you increase your chances of getting a truthful answer. Perhaps something did happen, or something is going on, in which case you have a decision to make. But if it didn't, or it isn't, you could be accused of lack of trust, and a whole new cause of argument could emerge. Marshall the facts, talk it through, and, if you need it, turn to the Help section.

Mobile phones and texting

There are some people who see the mobile phone as an extension of their arm: take it away and they are lost. There is no doubt that mobiles have become an indispensable aid to most people. Teenagers, in one survey, said that they would miss their mobile phones more than television. But if they are a marvellous aid to living, they are also susceptible to snooping; and the effects of that can be devastating. Deny your beloved any access to your phone, guard it jealously at all times – and he or she will immediately be suspicious. But if you leave it lying around, you'd better have a squeaky-clean conscience. Of people surveyed, 33 per cent of women and 30 per cent of men admitted snooping on their partner's phone correspondence. Thirty-eight per cent of respondents under 25, and 29 per cent of all respondents, said they had

M

checked their significant other's digital correspondence. A phone was the downfall of Tiger Woods, as well as countless other celebs and non-celebs, and the same thing could happen to you.

America, where mobiles caught on earlier than in Britain, is aware of the risks. The *New York Times* calls texting 'the new lipstick on the collar', that little slip that gives you away to a suspicious partner. Being found out by a partner checking on digital correspondence is not the only source of trouble: letters to advice lines complain of mobile phones ringing during sex and even being answered mid-intercourse. Not without reason are Blackberries becoming known as Crack-berries. There is no excuse for keeping your phone switched on during intimate moments, unless you're a surgeon on call or in MI5. If you do leave it on, you are, in a sense, indulging in group sex, because others can intrude into what should be two people alone. And if your new man or woman is constantly checking their phone, beware! They may be phone addicts, or simply ill-mannered louts.

Although mobiles are a wonderful way of keeping in touch they can also be misused. Continually ringing or texting can become irritating, especially at work, or in the pub with friends. Text messages can also be fired off in haste, and before proper thought. So use your phone wisely and not too well (*see also* Snooping, and Emails).

TEN REASONS WHY HE DIDN'T IMMEDIATELY ANSWER YOUR TEXT

1. It was the 17th you'd sent that day.
2. He's on the loo.
3. He never wants to see you again.
4. He's lost his phone.
5. You sent it to the wrong number.
6. He's working.
7. He can't decide what to say.
8. He's coming over, so what's the point?
9. He can't stop laughing long enough to text you back.
10. Unlike you, he has a life.

Money

Right from the first date, money is an issue. Do you offer to go Dutch or let the one who issued the invitation pay? Who earns the most? Should they take a bigger share of the expense? Who decides what you spend? Where does money go exactly?

A good rule is that the person who issues the invitation does the paying. If you're the guest, it's a nice gesture to offer to share the bill, but if you get a firm 'No', don't push it. Say

M

'My turn next time,' if a further meeting has already been discussed. If it hasn't, and you don't want to seem as though you're assuming another meeting, a simple 'Thank you' is enough. If meetings become regular events, then of course you should pay your way, unless one of you has had a windfall, in which case acceptance of a treat is in order. And even if you're the guest of a millionaire, don't opt for the most expensive items on a menu, whether or not you like them. You don't need to scour it for whatever is cheapest, but there's a happy medium.

If you're able to talk things through, money won't be an issue. You may even slip into handling your joint finances easily as well. Perhaps take turn and turn about, or accept gracefully where one or the other had a bonus. If money is a constant irritation, you need to look at how well you handle discussion. That's where the problem lies, not in your pocket (see Talking).

In a long-term relationship, money is too important to be left to chance. Unfortunately, when we fall in love, meaningful discussions about money seem almost obscene. That doesn't stop them being necessary. If you have an agreed strategy, arguments and resentment are less likely. It's unwise to assume that all money will be communal money. Each partner has a right to something of their own, to waste if they choose; and, if they have been used to financial independence, they may still wish to retain an element of it. Decisions on money jointly saved should be jointly made. A relationship is not a business, but it still needs boardroom discussion. However much love there is, you need to use your head. Saying 'I don't care about the money,' is not enough. If you want things to run smoothly, learn to care.

Monogamy

Before the 18th century, love didn't usually enter into relationships. They were made for practical reasons: money, land, position, status. Once the relationship was settled, men could stray as often as they liked; women were to remain faithful unto death. The age of the romantics ushered in monogamy: one man plus one woman = perpetual bliss. Except that fidelity was still expected only of the woman. The man could stray – it was almost expected of him – but the woman must stay within the nest.

The feminist revolution of the 1960s gave women the same right to stray as men, but at the same time suggested that men too should be faithful. That's how it is today: men and women choose whether or not to be monogamous – one man, one woman – or to have an open relationship. Recent research in Sweden suggests that there may be a 'divorce gene'

M

prevalent in men. In other words, for some monogamy is harder than for others. The fact remains that if one-man-one-woman works, and works well, it is the happiest possible solution for both partners.

Mood

If you're contemplating a 'momentous moment', be it a romantic proposal or raising a bone of contention, then pick your moment. The mood in which you make a request or lodge a complaint is crucial. You can do a lot to set a mood: a nice meal, soft music, an absence of belly-aching about the day or the in-laws . . . all these things affect the atmosphere. If you want to succeed in something, even a gentle seduction, mood is all-important. Disregard it at your peril.

Moving in

If you've talked it over and feel you know one another well enough to be sure of what you're doing, it can seem to make sense to move in together. But living together is very different from dating. However well you know one another, life together 24/7 can throw up some surprising revelations. You share a home not only with a partner, you share it with their family, friends, pets, colleagues, and idiosyncrasies.

If possible, keep both apartments going for a few weeks. This not only allows room to manoeuvre, it takes away that 'burned bridges' feeling, and allows you to relax. Knowing you have somewhere to go back to can make all the difference. The woman who is sweet reason in the cocktail bar may be a different proposition when it comes to who cleans the loo. If it's your place that will become the shared residence, accept that it is no longer 'your' place. You must accept change, not only in the surroundings but in house rules. Agree these in advance. If possible have two television sets, two radios. Establish a system for baths and showers; always being the one who finds the water cold is no fun.

Above all, accept that everyone needs their own company sometimes. Make sure there's plenty of storage space, and make advance agreements on who does what. Your mother may have fed you tit-bits while you watched the telly; your girlfriend is unlikely to do so. And the woman who welcomes your friends in the pub may feel differently when four of these same friends are raiding the fridge for tinnies at midnight. Work out money beforehand, and mutually agree some house rules. After that, all you can do is pray.

HE SAYS: Man is incomplete until he's married — and then he's finished.

> *SHE SAYS: 'If a body meet a body lying in the rye', you can be sure crops will be the last thing on their minds.*

HE SAYS: Roughly speaking, the female half of the workforce divides into two: the Desperate and the Politically Correct. The first lot spend their day emailing anything in trousers to say they've got tickets for Jamie Cullum, and would he like to go; the second lot positively angle for a chance to slap a man down.

> *SHE SAYS: It's not that men are selfish, it's just that in a one-TV household a woman must wait until she's widowed to discover that there's more to life than the Sports channel.*

HE SAYS: Have you ever been taken into the middle of La Perla, and then deserted? There's knickers right and left of you, and twenty women between you and the door.

> *SHE SAYS: You go out at Christmas to buy for your large combined families, and when you come out of the first shop he says hopefully, 'Is that it, then?'*

N

Negativity

Caution can be a virtue. It can also be a pain. If you're the person who always sees the risk, the cloud's black lining, the inevitable come-back, you need to ask whether or not you have developed a negative personality. I'm not suggesting you say yes to every suggestion; but, even when you see a snag, try to explore the possibilities first before you put the damper on it.

No for an answer

Sometimes we all have to deal with the man or woman who won't take no for an answer. When it's someone who has decided that you are their dream object, and they're someone you couldn't fancy on a desert isle without a ship in sight, you need to be firm but polite. Inventing another lover is

N

tempting, but the really persistent suitor will soon ferret out that that's a myth. Why not say or write, 'I like you as a person but we are not suited to be lovers, so there is no future in it. You have a lot to offer, and I don't want you to waste your time, which is why I'm telling you now.' Said in the right tone of disinterest that should work.

Nostalgia

Why do so many people flock to Friends Reunited or write to agony aunts asking how to trace that boy or girl who shared their first kiss? They do it because they've convinced themselves that that boy or girl was *the one*. In reality, they're trying to recapture the magic of first love, of being seventeen and that first heady excitement of sex and romance. In reality, that boy or girl can't have been so marvellous: if they had been, you wouldn't have moved on from them. Now, they'll have aged as you have aged. Their appearance, their personalities, their very essence, will be different. In life there's very seldom any point in going back. The past is rose-coloured-spectacles land. Return to it at your peril.

Not tonight, Josephine

However strong the sexual attraction between you, there will come a time when one or the other doesn't want sex. Sometimes even a cuddle seems an imposition, but that's usually because you fear it will turn into full-blown sex, and you're not up for it. If you're the one who is temporarily turned-off, make it clear you love them to bits but not until tomorrow. If you're the one who was champing at the bit until you met resistance, try not to see it as rejection. It doesn't mean he or she has gone off you. Give him or her a hug, and then turn over for sleep and a dream of how good sex will be tomorrow. After all, it will be a roll-over.

HE SAYS: While Einstein was discovering relativity, a sliver of cleavage, a flash of thigh, could put him right off. If he hadn't battled on, he might never have found his Theory.

> *SHE SAYS: What does not impress a woman is being phoned after three months' silence by a guy who says, 'I've been thinking about you all night.' Translated, that means he hasn't had sex for six weeks and his book fell open at your page. Or, worse still, he's been through the other pages, and you're his last hope.*

HE SAYS: If, on a first date, she tells you her tortellini is to die for and she only lives to make puff pastry, then she sees herself in the kitchen, baby in the high-chair, toddler in the garden, and you in the office forty pounds overweight and slaving to pay for it all. Unless you, too, are broody, run like hell.

> *SHE SAYS: Be careful. If the first course is oysters and the main course sweetbreads, make a run for it. You are dessert.*

HE SAYS: For years you've scraped the mould off jam or fish paste, and never ailed a thing. Don't tell her this, or her scream will stop the shoppers in thirteen aisles.

Occasions

A special date is coming up, and in your heart you're wondering just what he or she is going to do to make it special. You listen hard for hints, worry over what to wear, imagine everything from the Orient Express to a golden coach with six white horses and all the neighbours open-mouthed in wonder. And then she says her mum's coming for a special dinner, or he comes home with garage flowers and a box of After Eights (his favourites). We've all been there, and the initial impulse is *kill*!

Of course, occasions should be celebrated, but building an extravagant dream is asking for a let-down. Let it be known that you feel a particular date is special, don't just drop hints. Ask for suggestions, and give your own. Be reasonable: it won't be special if one of you is wincing at the thought of the bill. Some occasions need family and friends, others are

O

for you two alone. Make it clear which category that particular date falls into, and be very aware of what would make it special for your lover as well as for you. After you've done the preparation, *enjoy*.

Organisation

Organisation is great. Over-organisation is not. We all know the man or woman who is always two steps ahead, who keeps a social calendar and regards their diary as the Holy Grail. The trouble with the highly organised person is that they tend to organise things to suit themselves. She will make sure she sees *her* friends regularly; *his* will get fitted in if and when there's a spare day. He will organise life for him and his partner around his sporting calendar, his mates' nights out. In other words, the partner who organises will gradually weed out any part of their partner's life that makes for uneasy running. They don't do this intentionally at first, but gradually it becomes the norm. Unless their partner is apathetic about their own life and happy to go along, it can lead to rows, and ultimately to a split.

Recent research in America found that it was detrimental to any relationship if either partner's life was gradually downgraded in this way. We all need space sometimes, to bellyache to an old friend, to visit the gym or the salon. Above all, we need to feel we can be spontaneous if we want to be. Too rigid a social diary in the hands of one person imposes controls that can eliminate spontaneity, and that's bad. Nothing is less attractive than a domineering husband or a controlling wife. A partner can go along with what is organised, but inside they may be filled with resentment. There is even evidence to suggest that having their life over-organised can lead to erectile dysfunction in men.

If a man or woman feels their partner must be included in every aspect of their lives, it can feel for that partner like a loss of their individuality. And don't we all wince when someone says, 'I'll have to ask.'

As for the one who controls, if they have taken over the management of every area in life, then an unexpected event, the advent of an old friend or the need to stay over at the office, can feel like a threat to their authority. Even if they took that authority for themselves, it still hurts to have it threatened. Better to aim for a degree of mutual organisation, with inbuilt space for each partner to have room to breathe.

O

Orgasm

There is no one formula for bringing a partner, or indeed yourself, to orgasm. The psychologists Abramson and Pinkerton defined it in their book *With Pleasure: Thoughts on the Nature of Human Sexuality*. They said: 'The experience of sexual pleasure begins when the skin receptors in one or more erogenous zones are stimulated, and ends with a positive evaluation within the brain that the sensations experienced are indeed both pleasurable and sexual in nature.' Which is a long way of saying an orgasm needs a lead-up to it, and the more intense and prolonged that lead-up the more intense the orgasm.

I would add that, as well as what is going on physically, there should be some mental stimulation. Thinking of your lover, of the way you will feel on his or her arrival, imagining what you will say and do then, can all add to the build-up necessary for climax. But making orgasm too important, something you strain towards rather than joyfully anticipate, is not a good idea. So relax and enjoy, and if you have worries don't hesitate to ask for help (see Help section; *see also* Sex).

Ouch

For all of us there comes a moment when we put our foot in it. These slips are called social *faux pas*, and the mere memory of one can send shivers down your spine. So how do you handle them?

First of all, accept that the people listening to you, the people who heard you slip up, will probably be sympathetic. They will easily imagine being in your shoes, and they'll want to help you cover your blunder. If they're not sympathetic, then, in all probability, they have problems of their own. They're looking for an affront, and you've supplied one. If not this, it would have been something else. One way of dealing with a *faux pas* is to simply ignore it. Carry serenely on, leaving your listeners wondering if they really heard what they thought they did. Alternatively, you can apologise: 'I'm sorry. That was stupid,' will usually do it. If you're good at jokes, make a joke at your own expense. Most people will forgive you anything if you make them laugh. Remember that no one else is likely to care about your mistake as much as you care. Conversations move on, people have their own concerns to worry about. They're not going to concentrate on your mistake, so ignore it or apologise, or turn it into a joke, and then move on.

And don't feel that that *faux pas*, or your being caught

O

napping in some way, has ruined everything. Seeing someone fumble things can arouse protective feelings that may eventually translate into something more. A study carried out in California revealed that people who blush or embarrass easily are considered more trustworthy and generous than others. In other words, people feel safer with them because they don't seem adept at hiding their feelings. They're not perfect. The study, published in the *Journal of Personality and Social Psychology*, found that being easily embarrassed was regarded as 'pro-social', and made people feel more comfortable and trusting around one. Matthew Feinberg, one of the co-authors said: 'Our data suggests embarrassment is a good thing, not something you should fight.' The same goes for tears, even in men. Once upon a time, a weeping man was an object of derision. That's why the stiff upper lip was invented. Well, according to new research, opinions have changed. The American *Journal of Psychology of Men & Masculinity* published a survey of 150 college footballers with an average age of 19, which showed that 'Football players who strive to be emotionally expressive are more likely to have a mental edge on and off the field.' They were also thought to have higher self-esteem – in other words, they dared to cry instead of conforming to typical male gender roles that expect them to show little emotion and affection in front of other men. So, men, if you do a Rooney and cry tears of frustration, do it with your head held high.

SHE SAYS: *If it's you who is dieting, don't expect him to share your plain boiled cabbage. Nor should you give him a piled plate of fry-up and serve yourself shredded fennel. Sharing a meal is meant to be a joy, not a guilt trip.*

> HE SAYS: *In real life, parties fall into two categories: private and grand. Believe me, they're different! For the private party, there's the BYOB dilemma: you buy a bottle, then decide it isn't good enough, go back and buy another. By the fourth bottle you have something so expensive it merits Securicor, and you're worried they'll think you're a pretentious git.*

SHE SAYS: *Men can be divided into three categories: Bachelors, Husbands and Drivers. There's something about a long, shiny bonnet that twangs a man's cerebral cortex. Men have five different Y chromosomes, each paired to its own X. This makes them susceptible to the smell of petrol.*

> HE SAYS: *Your best friend is blunt: 'Move on. There are better fish in the sea.' This is like advising Captain Ahab to ignore the whale and settle for pilchards.*

HE SAYS: Women have often betrayed men, but they kept it quiet because they were ashamed of it. Men might boast, but women had more grace. Now they'll happily tell the tabloids how many lays they've had this week.

> SHE SAYS: It's a fuck-me dress and, judging from the crowd of men around her, that could be a self-fulfilling prophecy. She has fabulous hair: carrot-red and abundant enough for her to keep flicking it back. You hate her with a passion, especially when you realise she is pale gold and smooth all over.

HE SAYS: Don't drink if you want to know you're having a good time.

> SHE SAYS: Beware of dating accountants – they check everything. Numbers of stairs, organ pipes, birds on a picket fence: an accountant can accompany you to the check-out and tell you the bill will be £87.40. He's never wrong.

HE SAYS: Nowadays it's women who yell 'Get 'em off!' as male strippers gyrate. Men sit impassive before lap-dancers. You may drool a bit, but you keep your hands clenched (or in your pocket). Women grab – and guess what's most available.

Photographs

It's natural to want to capture special moments in life. We all want mementoes of happy moments, but there's another type of photograph, to which we need to give thought. Sexually explicit photographs are fine between lovers who will be together forever. But not all relationships last a lifetime. If you don't want embarrassing photographs to surface at a later date, think twice before you allow them to be taken and that you make very sure to get them back or destroyed if there's a break-up. Since so many photos remain within the mobile phones on which they were taken, that's not easy: a snap that was meant to be seen only by your lover can be round the world in seconds. In the hands of an unscrupulous person, it can become a weapon. A sensible person will understand the need for caution, so beware the lover who makes photos a condition, or scorns you for wanting safeguards.

P

Pity

When you're a child, turning on the waterworks is effective. People want to kiss you better, or give you sweeties. When you're grown up, it doesn't work, and if it does it's for the wrong reasons.

If you're heart-broken because your beloved has told you it's over, it's tempting to break down and cry, take to your bed, rend your clothes, and generally look as though you're about to expire. It's tempting to send the email that says, 'I can't go on without you,' or 'My heart is broken. Without you I have no future.' Don't do it.

Generally, ex-lovers don't return because they're sorry for you, and if they do, it doesn't last. They will never settle back into the relationship, and eventually they may accuse you of blackmailing them into a return. Far better to lick your wounds (see Licking Your Wounds) and get on with life. Let the one who deserted you see that, although wounded, you are far from down and out. They may heave a sigh of relief, and move on. They could also admire your courage and begin to re-evaluate the reasons for the split. Where pity doesn't work, admiration might.

Pornography

Once upon a time, pornography came in a brown-paper cover, furtively passed from one person to another. The advent of the internet changed all that. The world's biggest porn site claims 32 million users every month; more than 28,000 people are viewing porn every second; and recently many, many divorces cite porn viewing as a factor. Thirty-three per cent of men admit to viewing porn on line at work, and 1.4 million women look at porn each year. There are a reported 2.5 million porn sites, and 'homemade' sites featuring real sex and real people are being added all the time.

Pornography is defined as the explicit portrayal of sexual subject matter for the purposes of sexual arousal and erotic satisfaction. It has always existed, even in cave drawings from prehistoric times. The present easy access to it online, however, is causing a great deal of distress and insecurity. Hardcore porn features explicit sexual acts such as vaginal or anal penetration, cunnilingus, fellatio, ejaculation, and extreme fetish acts. Some of it can be bestial or violent and abusive, and is to be deplored. Softcore pornography usually takes the form of photographs, often displayed in magazines or on the internet or films. Where sexual acts are performed for a live audience, it is not termed pornographic, and

P

portrayals such as sex shows and striptease are not classified as pornography. The introduction of home videos and the internet saw booms in a porn industry that today generates billions of dollars a year worldwide.

Distress is arising in many relationships because one partner has virtually become a porn addict, spending hours at the computer which would be better spent in real sex with a live partner. A 2001 study of more than 7,000 adults in America found that 75 per cent admitted to masturbating while viewing pornography online, and there are nearly 300 million pages of porn online.

We all have curiosity about the sex act, but when looking at it becomes more enjoyable than indulging in it, questions need to be asked. Pornography addiction is a dependence characterised by obsessive viewing, reading, and thinking about often deviant sexual themes, almost to the exclusion of other areas of life. The reason why it is causing a lot of insecurity is that, once upon a time, sex was something we just got on with. Yes, we may not have been very expert but, because there was nothing with which to compare it, on the whole people were reasonably satisfied with their performance. Now that there is so much explicit discussion and viewing of the sex act, we are beginning to think that if we are not swinging naked from the chandelier we are missing out.

The worries that have been articulated to me are:

- Frequent viewing of extreme acts may make ordinary sex seem humdrum.
- Both men and women may worry that their bodies cannot measure up to the bodies of porn stars. The craze for extreme waxing is probably due to the smooth hairless bodies of the porn stars.
- Anxieties like this can spoil sex, even leading to an inability to reach orgasm.
- Partners may feel rejected, that the relationship has taken second place to porn.
- If children have access to pornography at an early stage, it may colour their attitude to real sex, and make it difficult for them to form normal relationships.
- For some it is seen as a form of infidelity. Others simply find it disgusting and turn against their partners.
- The more porn people watch, the more they want 'porn sex' as opposed to normal sexual intercourse so, in fact, it is shutting down imagination..
- It leads to men and women faking instant reactions similar to those in the pornography. This can lead partners to think there is no need for foreplay, and a vicious circle can begin.
- It encourages unsafe sex (i.e., sex without a condom).
- Frequent viewing can lead to wham, bam, thank you mam sex.

P

So who is in danger of becoming obsessed with porn? Most of us have curiosity that is easily satisfied, and leaves us unlikely to revisit porn sites. But to anyone who has had a repressed upbringing, in which sex was regarded as dirty, porn can be enormously exciting, the forbidden fruit. When a university wanted to research the effect of pornography on men, it failed to find enough men who had not viewed it to form a control group. If porn is affecting your life in any way, don't accept it as inevitable. Consult the Help section.

Pressure

Life today is stressful. Most of us are juggling home and jobs, or starting to ascend the career ladder, or merely working to keep our place on it. Money may be tight, or relationships rocky. Families can cause tensions. It's important to work out which pressures are unavoidable and which are self-induced. Do you need that new car, those shoes, that season ticket? Are any of those things worth the pressure? If the answer is yes, then shoulder the burden cheerfully. If it's something like childcare, and you need your job, then the pressure is unavoidable. But be careful what you take on. I've lost the count of the relationships I know of which have foundered because the strain of saving for a dream wedding became too much. If the pressure is time, list the areas of your life that require time, and then allocate what time you have. That way you'll be sure not to miss out on one area because you're so wrapped up in another. If there's a man or woman in your life, you can give them priority, but don't concentrate on them to such an extent that you forget friends, family, or, especially, me-time. You need a little of that to get your head straight.

Putting off

It's amazing how many relationships crumble in the aftermath of Christmas or the holiday season. This is because it's so easy to put things off 'till after'. And sometimes 'till after' can extend almost to the moment that you're walking down the aisle. Often putting off isn't fair. 'How could she dump me when we'd just had a good holiday?' is a legitimate question. The answer may be that the holiday failed to resolve the doubts that had been mounting up in her for months beforehand. By delaying the talking process 'till after', the ending is messy, and one partner is left feeling they've been used for a holiday and them dumped. So, don't fly off the handle without thought, but if something is really bugging you, if you have real doubts about your relationship, don't put off the end day. Get it out in the open and, hopefully, it can be sorted well before the holiday or the Christmas festivities.

HE SAYS: Men and women are different. Back in the 1970s when there was all that bra-burning, they tried to tell us there was no difference. Well, that's rubbish. We aspire differently. Women want commitment, even crave it. We accept it. Eventually. We even have different names for it. Women say they're 'in a relationship'. Notice that 'in' – you're in with them and the door's locked. Men say they're 'seeing' someone. Now you see it, now you don't. No doors. No keys.

Women want to understand *their man. A man doesn't need to understand a woman if he loves her. Men can be with a woman for forty years and be no wiser. Men don't want to change their woman, but women are dedicated to changing their men. It doesn't make sense. It's like buying a Paul Smith suit and then cutting it up for vest and shorts. Expect interference, house rules: no more keeping ale in the bath or cutting your toenails in front of the telly. No more nights out with the lads which turn into days. No more sitting up all night to see the World Heavyweight Contest. Go into any pub, and you can pick out the committed men: clock-watching, answering their phones every five minutes, downing their beer in a gulp because there's a casserole in the oven. Some of them have bunches of flowers with them. Before you can have a swift half with your mates you have to buy a sacrifice to the goddess of the home. How's that for oppression?*

And a woman doesn't have much tolerance for male pursuits. Unless she's your mother. Then she lets you keep your Scalextric in the front room, and your maggots in the fridge. Would a wife do that?

Que sera sera *(whatever will be, will be)*

Although there is much you can do to identify, and then encourage, a relationship, there is no denying that bringing it to fruition or preventing its break-up is not altogether in your control. As the songs says, 'What will be, will be,'(see Breaking Up). Try to see what has happened as part of life's pattern, something that was meant to be, rather than any failure on your part. And sometimes that thing you regard as a disaster may merely be clearing away what is not 100 per cent right in order that something better has room to grow.

SHE SAYS: The last man to admit a mistake was Pontius Pilate, and he washed his hands of it.

> *HE SAYS: Giving nature a helping hand is one thing; looking like the Dulux colour card is quite another.*

SHE SAYS: The reason men have small taut bottoms is that they sit on them all the time and the flesh compacts. (Not many people know that.)

> *HE SAYS: How many muscles does it take to put a lavatory seat down – and do they need to scream at you to come and do it for them? Have you really invaded their space by peeing standing up?*

SHE SAYS: Men have a mania for barbecues, and feed you raw meat in a charred coating that smells of smoke. For the next four hours you keep checking your watch to see what time the salmonella will strike.

> *HE SAYS: He comes back from a hot date, and the most he'll say is 'It was OK.' Next month you'll be at Moss Bros getting kitted out because her mother wants the wedding in the Leatherhead Gazette, but there's no need to chew it over now: not when Lineker's on the box.*

R

Rebound

It's common to get involved in a new relationship too soon after the end of another. Sometimes it's simply to ease that aching void in your heart. Sometimes it's to show the world you're not broken by being dumped. It may be simply to show your ex that you can still attract. Most likely it will be to prove to yourself that you are still desirable.

You need to be very careful about rebound relationships. Are you being fair to yourself, and, importantly, are you being fair to the new man or woman, promising something you ultimately won't be able to deliver? Better to simply begin a friendship, and give yourself space to recover before it turns into something more.

R

Relationships

No two relationships are the same, and you need to remember that. However, most relationships follow a fairly similar pattern. The first few weeks and early months are heady and exciting. Sex, if it's begun, is frequent and wonderful, you're probably unable to keep your hands off him or her. Life is exciting because, whatever you're doing at work or home, you're looking forward to seeing 'the one'. You find yourself thinking about your partner a lot. You're both on your best behaviour. Obviously living at top doh like that can't go on for ever. Gradually things settle down. You have agreed a degree of commitment and feel contented.

The second stage can last from the first couple of months to a year or more. You've both relaxed, and bad habits may have popped into view, but you're willing to compromise to make the relationship work. You may even have moved in together, completely or on an *ad hoc* basis. In the third stage, if you've got this far, you're deeper into commitment, but feel safe enough to argue your point, even have a good row. You can be yourself with your partner.

Obviously that's the description of an ideal relationship. Most have hiccups along the way. If they're handled honestly, and with mutual effort, the relationship can survive and last. If they become too frequent, it's time to talk, with a third party such as Relate, perhaps. Even if the relationship folds,

R

you carry from it valuable experience that will equip you to find that lasting relationship you crave.

Sometimes relationships simply come to an end. No one has failed, no one is to blame, it is simply the natural end of something that once was splendid but now has run out of steam. It's easy to feel you have failed, or to blame your partner. Regrets pile up. If only you had done, said, understood more, all would have been well. Although you may not see it at the time, this is a door closing on failure and opening to opportunity. Don't look back through rose-tinted spectacles; remember the rows as well as the love-ins. Try to be civilised about the parting; and if you feel aggrieved, remember that being happier without a partner than you were with one is the greatest revenge of all

Religion

Like class and cultural differences, religion can be divisive, often owing to family pressure. But, like the other two, where two people are determined to overcome obstacles, can compromise, and consider one another's feelings, all obstacles can be overcome. There are agencies that exist especially to help with this (see Help section; *see also* Class Divide).

R

Revenge

Revenge has formed the plot of many a novel. In real life we've seen it in every form. Remember the wronged wife who cut off all her husband's trouser legs, or the spurned lover who secreted prawns in a curtain rod and drove her lover from his flat as the stench escalated. But revenge is only momentarily satisfying. Afterwards there are consequences. One of them is that, unless you have been very cunning, you look a fool. If you have gone too far, you could face criminal prosecution. In any event, you have run up a signal that the man or woman who betrayed you is still the most important person in your life, the focus of all your thoughts. If your anger is directed towards a Love Rat, you can be very sure that he or she will absolutely love the fact that they are still pulling your strings.

Walk away, head held high, and achieve happiness. To show how little the loss of them affected your life is the best revenge of all.

Romance

We all need a little romance in our lives, and too often we have to find it in the cinema or in the pages of a book. It doesn't cost anything to write a love note to a partner, and leave it for them to find. Bringing in a rose from the garden for your partner can warm the heart. Catching their eye across the room at a party and giving them that 'Much more later,' look can set the pulses racing. Saying, 'You know I can't say things like that,' is abrogating your responsibilities. So is thinking that the fact that you're putting his dinner on the table obviates the need to kiss him stupid beforehand. I don't know why so many people are reluctant to display their romantic side. I promise you, the dividends if you do are huge.

Romance fraud

Criminals using the internet and dating sites to commit fraud is a worldwide problem. Recent research suggests there may be as many as 200,000 cases. Often the fraudsters are working in teams based outside Britain, and romance fraudsters are skilful at building up a picture of an attractive person with much to offer. They take their time to establish a friendship, and then the process of extracting cash or gifts begins. Britain's serious crime squad is aware of the problem, and considers it to be organised crime. The fraudsters are willing to spend time grooming victims because they probably have many victims on the hook at the same time, some of them already handing over cash. A frequent ploy is to say how much they would like to meet in person, but

R

their cash is tied up until they get to Britain. If the money can be advanced to them, they say, they will repay it as soon as you meet face to face – a meeting that will never occur. This does not mean that you should avoid the internet and dating sites altogether. It does mean that you need to be immensely cautious about parting with money until you know a person through and through, have met their family, friends and colleagues, and know their address and identity. *See also* Internet Dating.

TEN WAYS TO SPOT A LOVE RAT, MALE OR FEMALE.

1. He/she smiles a lot.
2. He/she's more attentive than usual, especially sexually.
3. He/she avoids your eye or tends to almost stare you out.
4. You feel uneasy.
5. He/she guards their phone, or leaves the room to take calls.
6. You seldom or never meet their friends.
7. They don't seem to have friends.
8. They always have a ready answer, no matter what the question.
9. They insist they told you something when you know they didn't.
10. They rinse an item of clothing they'd normally put in the wash box.

Running him/her down

It makes you feel big and secure in your relationship. 'He's such an idiot. I can't trust him to boil an egg.' Or 'She doesn't understand, the game goes straight over her head.' Remarks like these are accompanied by a knowing smile that says, 'Yes, he/she's an idiot, and I'm a saint for putting up with them.' Listen to a group of women, and you'd think they were all married to morons. For centuries men have been happy to suggest their women were empty-headed. Now women are doing it too.

A little mockery may be harmless enough, but sometimes it can go too far, and what is revealed is real and personal. Celebrities do it, describing their partners as idiots or wimps for a cheap laugh. Others will display themselves in a way they know is embarrassing to their partners. Psychologists will tell you that belittling your partner betrays an inner dissatisfaction with your relationship, a desire to exert control and appear in charge. Whatever the reason, if you spend a night with your friends making fun of your partner, it doesn't make for good sex when you get home. Inch by inch you are chipping away at the respect you should, indeed need, to feel for your partner. The odd joke at your partner's expense is fine. But when it becomes your only script it's not only wrong, it's unfair. Even when the relationship is over, it's best to spare the detail of what an utter wuss he or she was.

SHE SAYS: Promises are like flowers and ice cream. They have a limited shelf life.

>*HE SAYS: Speed-dating sucks. You circle a room, spending three minutes with each woman – three minutes: not enough time for a fruit fly to orgasm. If you chat well she ticks your box. Big deal.*

SHE SAYS: Speed-dating is a waste of time. After you've binned the Lecher, the Mother's Boy, the Mute, the Boaster and the Christopher Lee Look-alike, you totter off home to lie down in a darkened room. Anyone who hopes to find anything with a pulse in three-minute bites must be daft or desperate.

>*HE SAYS: She says, 'What are your interests?' and what springs to mind is, 'Getting out of here.' Or 'Your bed or mine?' Of course you don't say that. You say you're interested in politics, eating out, and modern jazz.*

SHE SAYS: 'What you've never had, you never miss,' is a cliché invented by sadists to confuse the issue. What you've never had achieves a perfection no real romance could aspire to. Unrequited love is, by its very nature, flawless, and you are landed with it. All you can do is hang in there.

Saying sorry

They say an average Britain says sorry at least eight times a day. That's nearly 3,000 times a year and zillions in a lifetime. Used properly, 'sorry' is a lovely word, conveying courtesy and a sense of the other person's rights as well as your own. When you're saying 'sorry' too often, however, it can be a sign of low self-esteem, of an uncertainty about your right to your own space. If you're one of those people who seem to be apologising simply for being alive, look at the Help section. And if there's someone in your life who expects too frequent apologies, or makes you question yourself too intensely, you have some serious thinking to do.

Sometimes apologies, however hard to make, are necessary. Occasionally, even when they're undeserved, they're advisable. But don't make them simply to produce peace – that seldom works, because you'll harbour resentment.

S

However, if you make a considered decision to apologise, don't then see it as weakness. Restoring harmony with a thoughtful apology is an act of strength. Why continue in a state of siege when one simple word could end it all? Pride is a cold bedfellow, especially when that same five-letter word may be trembling on your partner's lips.

Second time around

Second-time-around comes complete with baggage. That is inevitable. If you are supremely confident, you accept all that the relationship has to offer, and rise above the drawbacks. If you are at all insecure, the thought that you are walking in someone else's footsteps can bring you down. Remember you were chosen for yourself, not as a substitute. What you have together is alive; the only thing that can spoil it is allowing the past to intrude. That past is dead and has only the power you choose to give to it (*see* Baggage).

Self-esteem

It's impossible to be at ease in a relationship unless you have regard and affection for yourself. This is very different from arrogance or self-satisfaction, which are unattractive qualities. I'm talking about feeling that you have a right to be alive, and an expectation that other people, whether or not they like you, will not be hostile towards you.

These questions will help you to work out whether or not you suffer from low self-esteem:

♥ Do you suffer from agonies of anxiety before social occasions?
♥ Are you always afraid people will think badly of you?
♥ Do you comfort-eat, or have a tendency to other food issues?
♥ Do you fear for the future?
♥ If someone pays you a compliment, do you think they're only saying it to be kind?
♥ Do you have a constant feeling that things are going to go wrong?
♥ Do you avoid challenges, for instance applying for promotion?
♥ Do you have a low expectation of your future?
♥ Do you see sex as a sign that you are needed and wanted, and fret if it's not always available?

If you answered Yes to most of these questions, turn to the Help section.

S

Sometimes a partner, loving and supportive in many ways, can inadvertently make you feel a failure. He's a champion ballroom dancer, you have two left feet. She reads (and understands) Martin Amis, you struggle with *Viz*. He can charm complete strangers, you're hardly at ease with your cousins. You know how it is – you love him or her because they're special, but it makes you feel a failure. When that happens, list what you bring to the relationship. Are you the one who remembers dates, keeps fridge and freezer stocked, keeps an eye on the money, or can mend a plug? Find your own thing to excel in, and make sure the two of you function as a double act occasionally. And if all else fails, remember that that super-he or she chose you. That makes you pretty special.

If you feel your partner is unhappy in the relationship, consider that the trouble may be their own lack of self-esteem. The person who is always out of sorts may secretly be asking, 'Am I truly loved?' or 'Does he love me more than his mum, his sister, his ex?' 'Would she drop me if someone better came along?' Outwardly they may seem confident, sociable, outgoing, but in the intimacy of a relationship that façade may drop to reveal someone emotionally insecure. Often it's owing to childhood trauma: bullying, sibling rivalry, being put down by parents. A sympathetic partner can help to heal those wounds. If not, see the Help section (*see also* Ego).

Sensuality

This is equally as important as sex, but some people are inclined to dismiss it. It's sometimes referred to as 'feeling sexy', and though it can be the result of a physical relationship, it is also aroused by pleasurable things: silk next to your skin; perfume; the touch of flower petals; water rippling against your limbs – anything that makes you feel relaxed and good is a sign that your sensuality is alive and well. So if the man or woman in your life isn't there, pamper yourself, and get the feel-good factor anyway.

Serial adultery

To find your lover has betrayed you once is bad enough. To find it has been a regular event is devastating. For some, probably most, people the answer is simple: walk out of the door. If you have children, or have been together for a while, it's not so easy. In all probability, the guilty party will apologise profusely and promise it will never, ever happen again. They'll woo you in every way and, if you permit it, the sex will be wonderful. But not wonderful enough to wipe out your pain.

Sometimes serial adulterers are driven by vanity: can I attract that man? Will that woman fall for me? I bet she will.

S

Sometimes they are driven by insecurity: am I still worth loving? Can I still pull? Some experts believe that childhood trauma, particularly the absence of a mother, creates a needy individual constantly searching for a love that he or she is incapable of giving back for any length of time. The 64,000-dollar question is, can they change? If they want to, and are prepared to undertake therapy, occasionally they can. But cures are just that, occasional; and their partner must live with the fear of a recurrence. If your lover is apt to stray, first explore your relationship for anything that might constitute a reason. If, in many ways, they are charming and good company – and they often are – then talk to Marriage Care or Relate to see if the relationship can be repaired (see Help section). If, after you've tried to see the whole picture, you are still in despair or consumed by doubt, then move on. The human heart is surprisingly resilient but, like everything else, it has its limits.

Sex

Scientists will tell you that sex is good for you. It increases the levels of the bonding hormone oxytocin, which strengthens a relationship. It benefits the heart, lowers blood pressure, burns 180 calories an hour, and reduces stress. It also feels good. However, when it comes to frequency and intensity, it's much harder to lay down rules or measure benefits. For some, sex is little more than a gentle cuddle, and an orgasm that resembles a good sigh. For others it needs to be tempestuous and leave both parties gasping for breath. Similarly, it is impossible to lay down rules on the frequency of love-making. In some African societies couples have sex on average 440 times a year. In Western countries, the average is around 120 times a year. For some it must be daily, even more than once a day. For others the perfect rhythm is weekly, even monthly. They're perfectly happy until someone confides that they are at it like knives, five times a night and still counting. That's when doubts creep in, and what was a perfectly satisfying sexual pattern can suddenly look like a poor substitute.

The right sexual pattern for you is the one that feels good. But in order to achieve this level of satisfaction, both partners need to have matching drives. If imbalance of desire is affecting your relationship, trained sexual counsellors can help to achieve compatibility (see Help section). Remember that desire can sometimes be affected by physical health or outside stress. Sex toys or frilly lingerie won't help if your libido is dulled by hormonal imbalance or illness. These need medical attention. Nor can the man or woman facing redundancy or financial ruin perform as though everything in the garden was rosy, although having sex can be a huge source of support in difficult times. The important thing to remember is that your sex life is *your* sex life. The pattern

S

must be designed by you, in tandem with your partner, and is not to be compared with what works for anyone else.

As for 'unusual' sexual practices, if they don't do physical harm and both partners are equally happy with them, they're OK. Used properly, sex enhances life. Misused or treated carelessly, it can create havoc. Embrace it; don't fear it; take the trouble to thoroughly understand it. It's amazing how many people have only a rudimentary understanding of their own bodies and sexuality. Sex is powerful – but don't see it as a panacea for all woes, nor the glue that can hold a disintegrating relationship together. Wonderful as it is, it should always be the icing on the cake – not the cake itself. Nor should celibacy, when it is by mutual desire, be regarded as the absence of love. Many deep and lasting relationships have been based on it. Some people, both men and women, will try to use sex as a bargaining tool to get what they want. This is a fairly despicable way to treat what is one of mankind's greatest gifts.

What happens when someone who longs for sexual fulfilment finds they can't perform? In women it may manifest itself as vaginismus, a painful tightening of the vaginal muscles that makes penetration impossible. In men, it is usually a failure to get an erection or, having got it, to maintain it. There can be a host of causes for both these conditions, both medical and psychological. The good news is that help is available, either through your GP or a trained sexual therapist. One cause may be anger or anxiety, particularly in the case of men: both conditions produce the hormone adrenalin, which causes the body to prepare for flight by diverting blood away from the extremities, including the penis. You start to worry about your failure, and that makes matters worse, causing a vicious circle. Anxiety can also occur if someone has been sexually inactive for a while, perhaps after bereavement, break-up, or divorce. This is where a patient lover, who realises that all sex does not have to be penetrative, can help enormously. But in this, as with any other sexual difficulty, remember that help is available if you reach for it (see Help section; *see also* Orgasm).

TEN THINGS THAT MAKE A MAN ATTRACTIVE
1. His smile
2. Clean finger nails
3. Good manners
4. A sense of purpose
5. Not looking like a tailor's dummy
6. Polished shoes
7. Good teeth, not too white
8. Smelling good but not reeking of cologne
9. A pleasant voice
10. A sense of humour

S

Sex Without Strings: Sometimes, after the end of a relationship, we shut down our feelings. We neither want nor could handle another relationship at the moment. Physical desire may remain, however, and it is tempting to think of having a purely sexual relationship, one that will satisfy physical needs without any danger of emotional involvement. Is there such a relationship? Undoubtedly there is, but whether or not it's wise to enter into one is another matter. Its modern name is Friends with Benefits, but that doesn't change the risks – nor the benefits, if handled correctly.

The trouble is that casual sex is seldom sex without drawbacks. Most people need sex to have some meaning, and can find meaningless sexual gratification a demeaning experience. You may also be kidding yourself: a survey of more than 800 supposedly casual sexual encounters found that 52 per cent of men and 50 per cent of women were actually hoping, not for a one-night stand, but for something that would lead to a more permanent relationship. The sex act has an effect on the chemistry of the brain. Dopamine is released and leads to an outpouring of bonding hormones. Before you know it, what was meant to be a brief encounter has taken on new meaning, for you – though it has not necessarily been the same for the other person involved. Result: complications, and not the neat and tidy release you hoped for. Of course, casual sex can occur, and some people can walk away satisfied and unscathed. But they tend to be the exception rather than the rule. And the walking away can suddenly fill you with the feeling you've been used, which is a bit unfair when you set out to be a user yourself. Repeated casual sex can lower your self-esteem, and with it comes the risk of infections, physical abuse, and even pregnancy. However, if you've thought it through, considered the risks, and prepared yourself so that you embark on it with a positive attitude, you may come through unscathed. Just don't think it's the perfect answer it can sometimes seem to be (*see also* Friends with Benefits aka Fuck-buddies).

Sexual history: At some stage in a relationship, the subject of previous partners will arise. If you've had even a mildly lurid past, the temptation is to lie. You certainly don't want to do a Cleggy and say 'Less than thirty', but if you don't tell the truth you move into dangerous territory. Trust is basic to a lasting relationship, and if your lie comes out at a later stage you'll have destroyed that trust. Better, I think, to suggest that the past, yours and theirs, should remain undisturbed unless there is a compelling reason to reveal details. Of course, you risk arousing the suspicion that the number of your previous partners is so huge it doesn't bear telling, so if you have had a reasonable number of partners it could be easier to be honest. What is a reasonable number? A survey of sexual behaviour in

S

the UK, *The National Survey of Sexual Attitudes and Lifestyles*, revealed that women had an average of 6.5 sex partners and only 19.4 per cent had had ten or more. The same survey showed that 34.6 per cent of men have had more than ten sexual partners, and the average number is 12.7. If you are within reach of the norm, and feel comfortable with it, you are entitled to speak out. You are also entitled to keep even reasonable behaviour to yourself.

Why do some people feel the need to know the number of those who have gone before them? It may be idle curiosity, but more likely it stems from insecurity: 'Does he or she know more about making love than I do, and if so, will I disappoint?' It amazes me that so many people are insecure about their sexual prowess, but the fact remains that they are. Some people may fear their being just one more scalp on a hunter's belt, but beware someone who takes a compulsive interest in your sexual history. A lover should accept you as you are now. If they have a compelling need to dig and dig, you are entitled to question their motives.

Sexual compatibility: Sometimes two people who are well-matched in every other way will find that they differ greatly in sexual desire. One partner may like to be experimental, the other prefers to be traditional. In the first flush of love the traditionalist consents to 27 different positions and the odd bit of bondage, but in time variety palls. He or she wants leisurely sex, and probably even less of that. The result is a constant tug of war between differing expectations and abilities. If both sides are prepared to give a little, they can each gain from the other. The traditionalist expands his or her horizons; the experimentalist learns how pleasant it can be to take time and enjoy well-trodden paths.

Easy access to porn has helped to create a feeling that sex must be hyper and athletic, whereas good sex should be all about mutual pleasure. And although the good lover should always be ready to learn, making love while thumbing the pages of the Kama Sutra is not to be recommended. So, if your sexual preferences are incompatible, what should you do? First of all, talk to one another. Better still, show what you need and what you have to offer. And if talking fails, turn to Relate's trained sexual therapists (see Help section; *see also* Libido).

Sexually transmitted diseases: Sexually transmitted diseases, also known as sexually transmitted infections, have been around since the dawn of time, but it is a mistake to think that modern medicine has rendered them harmless. Yes, treatment has improved significantly, but for some STDs there is still no absolute cure. That's why it's important to take precautions when sleeping with someone whose sexual history is not completely known to you. Unprotected sex,

S

except with a long-term, faithful partner, is simply not worth the risk. There can be a significant probability of transmission of infection between humans by means of human sexual behaviour, including vaginal intercourse, oral sex, and anal sex. It's very easy to think that because someone is intelligent and considerate, they will be 'safe'. STDs can happen to the best of people, so outward appearance is irrelevant. Despite considerable progress, the UK still has a worrying sexual health record, with some of the worst sexually transmitted infection rates in Western Europe. There's been a steady increase, between 2008 and 2010, in diagnoses of chlamydia, gonorrhoea and herpes, and HIV is still one of the fastest-growing serious health conditions in the UK. If you are worried that you may have been infected, don't wait for symptoms. Contact your doctor or nearest genito-urinary clinic, and get the all-clear, or access to treatment.

Signs

If it were possible to list the incontrovertible signs that prove someone is attracted to you, or the equally incontrovertible signs that someone is cooling off, how much simpler life would be. Unfortunately, some people are too shy to reveal their feelings, others too devious to betray how they really feel, or are experts at pretending to emotions they don't feel. The only true signs that someone is attracted to you is that they make an effort to see you again, but if they make eye contact, are happy to sit closely, and are attentive to your comfort, you can be pretty sure they are not uninterested.

The signs that someone, once amorous, is cooling off are a little easier to spot. Reluctance to be intimate, long silences, short replies to questions, bursts of ill temper, long absences without contact . . . all these things can be danger signs. But they can also be signs that your partner or lover is under strain, so don't be too quick to draw conclusions. I'm tempted to say, 'Use your instinct,' but that again can be fallible. If you're a modest, self-effacing type, you will put down to imagination the signs that he or she is showing of being drawn to you. If you have quite an opinion of yourself, you may see signs of attraction where they don't exist. The modest one may imagine cooling off, because he or she is half-expecting it; the arrogant person won't see what's right under their nose.

Sleeping

Lack of sleep can be the death of a good relationship, so make sure you get your seven hours. If your lover is a restless sleeper or, heaven forbid, snores, don't lie there and suffer.

S

Conditions such as snoring or noisy dreaming can respond to treatment. Comforting as the double bed is, don't be afraid to sneak away after sex to seek refuge in the spare bedroom. A good night's sleep, and you'll be fresh enough to tiptoe back and share your lover's bed in the morning.

Small talk

There's a huge difference between chat-up lines and small talk. Small talk is important because it eases silences, might eventually lead to more serious talk, and, when it gets going, allows everyone to relax and find out whether or not they like one another. It should never be a gabble, the stream of almost nothing that you can get from people who make it seem as though the sky will fall if they shut up. But it needs to be plentiful enough to stimulate the listener into joining in. Making small talk to strangers requires courage, but it's worth it because it's a way of saying, 'I've noticed you. I like you, I hope you'll like me.'

Being good at small talk necessitates being sensitive to other people's reactions. If they look confused or bored, you need to change tack. If you're doing *all* the talking, you're not getting it right. If you ask a question, make it one that can't be answered with a Yes or No. 'Have you been to this party before?' might only elicit a one-word answer. 'I hardly know anyone here; do you know anyone? Have you been before?' should require them to join in. Saying 'I work in IT. Do you do something really interesting?' pays them a compliment and encourages them to talk about their work, which is a safe opener for most people. 'How did you get into that? Do you meet interesting people? Is it a big firm?'– the list of supplementary questions is endless.

Don't be afraid to admit weaknesses. 'I never know how to balance a glass and a plate,' usually brings a smile and an offer of help. If they tell you something praiseworthy, then praise them: nothing raises the temperature of a meeting like a compliment. 'That's a fab jacket,' will probably win you a friend for life. But it's also important to know when to end the small talk. If they seem disinterested, you can do better elsewhere. Say 'Lovely chatting to you. I expect we ought to mingle now,' and move on to a more appreciative audience.

Snooping

See Mobile Phones and Emails.

S

Social networking

One survey has found that, for the British people surveyed, being on Facebook is more important than a cup of tea, a shower, or perhaps most startlingly of all, a flushing toilet. The Science Museum in London conducted the survey by asking 3,000 adults what they couldn't live without. Facebook turned up in fifth place, beaten only by sunshine, the internet, drinking water, and a fridge. Facebook was also considered to be more important than having a mobile phone, Google, a flat-screen TV, a Wii console, an iPad, and Twitter. If, for some people, a social-networking site that was launched a mere seven years ago has become more important than drinking water, I think we have problems. According to the company, Facebook now has more than 750 million active users, and people spend more than 700 billion minutes on the site each month.

In a recent survey, one in five women admitted to having accessed their partner's emails or messages on social-networking services such as Facebook without their knowledge, compared to one in ten men. And the guilty snoopers admitted this had led to arguments. Despite this, a large proportion of couples trust each other with their online passwords, and the younger they are the more trusting they seem to be. Among those under 25, more than half shared their log-in credentials with their partner. In the 45-54 age bracket, only a third did so. But in the same survey, 34 per cent admitted to lies online, or creating a false identity. More than one in ten men and women admitted they had lied about their age; the second most popular areas for digital untruths were weight for women, and financial status for men. As that survey proves, social networking, if it is to have a happy outcome, needs caution. It is probably best to keep your password to yourself, but if you are in a loving relationship this can cause tension. 'What is he/she concealing, if I'm not to be trusted with the password?' The reverse of that is, 'Why is he/she so insistent on access? Don't they trust me?'

You also have to be careful of malicious postings. If you read something that upsets you, take time out before you respond or demand explanations. Unfortunately, social networking provides a wonderful opportunity for mischief, and even downright spite. It can also attract sick people, who find it amusing to make jokes about topics such as rape and murder. Petitions urging the removal of such pages have been signed by more than 3,600 people in the UK, and 175,000 people in the US. I worry, too, about the fact that most social-network site users are doing so in the comfort of their own home, which can create a false sense of security. You feel safe, and this can lead you to be too trustful of messages sent to

S

you. It can also lead you to reveal more than you should. Remember that you are not speaking to one other person in confidence; you are, in essence, speaking to the whole world. The wrong remark can be round the network in seconds, as many people have found to their cost. You think you are only speaking to your friends, but Facebook admits that hackers are breaking into hundreds of thousands of accounts every day in an attempt to access users' messages, photographs, and other personal information. Although not every attempt is successful, and Facebook is working hard to combat hacking, caution about what you do decide to put on line is vital. And, unfortunately, social-networking sites have made it easier than ever to cheat on your partner. It is relatively easy to keep fake accounts in addition to the one you're happy for your lover to see. It is not uncommon for Love Rats of both sexes to have several accounts, and more than one poor dupe on the go at any one time. It is also fairly common for that handsome guy or gal to whom you're spilling out your heart to actually be a teenager laughing their heads off at just how gullible the human race can be.

So approach social networking with care. It can enhance your life, widen your acquaintance, provide hours of enjoyment and friendship. It can also make you cry.

Space

However close a relationship may be, we all need space. In the first flash of sexual attraction, the desire is to bond with your beloved, to laugh when they laugh, cry when they cry, be in touch with them every minute of the day, or at least know where they are. This is fine for a short while, but the need for space can occur at different times for different people. Too many romances that could blossom given time die because one partner is too overpowering, too soon (*see* Dartboard).

TEN ATTRACTIVE QUALITIES IN A WOMAN
1. She smells nice.
2. She understands the offside rule.
3. Your mates like her.
4. She makes you laugh.
5. She likes a drink, but knows when to stop.
6. She doesn't mind getting messed up occasionally.
7. She understands the importance of mates.
8. She can take a joke.
9. There are bits of her she keeps for you alone.
10. You can see her bearing your children.

S

Spinning

From time immemorial, men and women have gone in for spinning. That's when you try to create a relationship where none exists. You lobby the object of your affection with texts and emails, manufacture opportunities to bump into them, arrange double dates if you can, and talk to anyone who will listen about how well you and X are getting on. You persuade friends to ask them to parties, or even throw a party of your own to which they're invited. You study their likes and dislikes, hobbies and other interests. Wherever they go, you're there. All the while you're buoyed up by hope. Sometimes it works – they get so used to you in their lives 24/7 that they begin to include you. More often, they simply move on, leaving you empty-handed. It can work, so perhaps it's worth a try – but don't spend much time or money on it. It simply isn't worth it.

Standards

Although I believe two people can be happy even though they don't have shared interests and are not obviously compatible, I think it is much harder, if not impossible, to be happy together without shared standards. By that I mean agreement on intolerable things such as homophobia or racism. Vegans can live happily with meat-eaters, the devout with atheists, as long as there is mutual respect, but don't ever let that initial flush of infatuation blind you to the real nature of your lover. Together for ever is a very long time (*see also* Compatibility).

Status

Once upon a time, men of substance were considered a good catch, and women aspired to 'marry up'. Now the sexes are almost identical in earning power, education, and career. Either can be the main breadwinner; house-husbands are no longer an eyebrow-raising rarity. But as men see their role as provider and master of the house diminish, they seem to be getting less willing to commit. Far from relishing decreased responsibility, they seem to want to avoid it altogether. Sociologists have identified this as a quest for protracted bachelorhood. Hopefully, the prospect of an equal partnership will prove more attractive in the long run. There is still a role for the supportive spouse, of whatever sex, however much the world has changed (*see also* Class Divide).

S

Stonewalling

You know the technique: they don't give you a yes or a no, they just stonewall. Perhaps it's over a wedding date, the moment to move house, to have a baby, to meet his or her folks. It's always 'some time', which you now tend to think is spelled 'never'. Pick your moment, not in the middle of a row, and ask for a deadline. When that day comes, and he or she doesn't deliver, accept it. They ain't going to. You know what to do: *move on*.

Sulking

If one partner sulks, it's difficult. If both do, it it's a dead end. Sulking is childish, an admission that you can't cope with arguing your case. How do you deal with a sulker? You can simply ignore it, keep on being pleasant, talking whether or not you get a reply, and generally behaving as though you were dealing with a naughty toddler who will stop his or her tantrum shortly.

You can issue an ultimatum – 'Snap out of it, or I go'– or you can cease to co-operate: stop doing your share of chores, and just get on with your own life. Though if you adopt this option, it's important to mention where you're going, and be sensible about speaking when necessary. What you mustn't do is start to sulk back. This can lead to a deadlock that can go on indefinitely.

If your partner is a sulker, don't argue about it, but choose a good moment to discuss the fact that it can't become a way of life. Try to make an agreement that, when angry, silence can be allowed only for a while, for time to cool off, and then there must be discussion. If you're the sulker, recognise your own inadequacy. Take that agreed breathing space, and then set out your case. Life is too short to fill with heavy silences.

S

Survival

When relationships go wrong, it can feel like the end of the world – and, in a way, it is. The end of one world (which may have been rocky for a while), and the chance of a new one. That is hard to believe at the time, so here are ten tips for ways to survive until you do see signs of rebirth.

♥ If you feel like it, simply do nothing for a while. But never for more than an hour.

♥ Cry if you want to. You may fear that if you start you won't stop. You will. Think about it – break-ups are common. How often do you see people walking around with hankies to their eyes?

♥ Exercise, even dancing to music on the telly, helps.

♥ Ring a help line. They're waiting for your call (see Help section).

♥ Write down how you feel.

♥ Give yourself small treats. Whatever grabs your fancy.

S

- Have a massage. It's a loving touch.

- Make a list of ten things you'd like to accomplish by Christmas.

- Go through your wardrobe, and put anything that reminds you of him or her out for Oxfam.

- Play music. 'Coming up Roses' and 'Viva España' are good to start with.

HE SAYS: If she even hints at the biological clock, scarper. You might get more than you bargain for.

> *SHE SAYS: You sit on the remote control, which is the only way of stopping them channel-hopping in love scenes. They don't understand the female need to see Brad's lips meet Angelina's, so, just as the noses touch – Zap! He's clicked to Sport on Four, and when you scream and bite the cushions, he gives one of those long, slow sighs: God!*

HE SAYS: Women are experts in the art of retaliation. They don't fist fight, but when it comes to passive resistance, they're ace. Ask for a drop of milk; you'll get just that: a drop. Lunch will be a tin and an opener (with condiments if you're lucky). They know how to wound, these women. But they still set the table and put out a flower arrangement. That's to rub salt into the wound.

> *SHE SAYS: You can have a good cry with a best friend, until she makes you laugh by telling you the other woman has an arse the size of the Albert Hall and shaves her moustache with a blow-torch. You both know it's lies, but it's friendly lies.*

Talking

Talking about problems has to be a two-way process, and that means that sometimes you have to stay silent even though what your partner is saying infuriates you. If you, or if he or she, keeps interrupting, you're not talking, you're arguing. Talking can often lead to solutions, so learn to do it right. Write down the points you want to make beforehand, and memorise them. You only need three or four; more than that can turn into a rant. Don't take the list with you. Above all, be prepared to listen and, when you can, inject a little humour into the situation. Not only must you be prepared to listen, but you must be prepared to change your mind if your partner's points make sense. This isn't backing down, it's facing facts. Talking about a problem in the immediate aftermath of a row is not a good idea. Let tempers cool before you do it, to have maximum chance of success. And if, after talking more than once, you're no nearer a solution, turn to a mediator, someone who will listen to you both and help you towards a fair conclusion (see Help section).

Termination

Terminating a pregnancy is a personal choice. There can be many medical and social reasons for so doing, but it is vital that the woman makes her choice free from coercion or pressure from anyone, which means even her partner. In Great Britain (England, Scotland and Wales), it is legally permissable for a termination to be carried out up to 24 weeks of pregnancy, unless there are exceptional circumstances. You may be able to have a termination after 24 weeks if your life is under serious threat, or if your baby will be born with a severe disability. Most terminations take place before 12 weeks of pregnancy. In Northern Ireland it is legal only in exceptional circumstances.

To have a termination you must get consent from two doctors. Usually, the first is your GP, and the second is from the clinic or hospital where it will take place. The two doctors must decide, on balance, that a termination will decrease any risks to your (or your child's) physical or mental health. You may be offered a choice of procedure, but this will depend on

T

how many weeks pregnant you are, and whether you have any pre-existing medical conditions.

There are two main types of termination – medical and surgical. Medical termination is often carried out in the early stages of pregnancy (up to nine weeks). It involves taking drugs to cause a miscarriage. You can, however, have a medical termination at a later stage. Surgical termination refers to two different procedures – vacuum aspiration, and dilation and evacuation (D&E). Vacuum aspiration is the commonest and is usually used if you are less than 15 weeks pregnant. D&E can be used if you are more than 15 weeks pregnant.

It is vitally important that any woman who has a termination is doing so because, after reflection, she has decided it is the best course for her. If possible, it's always best to have had some form of counselling beforehand, but that counselling must be impartial, setting out the pros and cons but leaving the woman free to make the final decision. If you have had a pregnancy terminated, and still have issues with your decision, or if you are contemplating termination, there are several organisations who will understand and help (*see* Help section).

T

Tolerance

There are certain areas where two competing wills are almost bound to clash. It can begin with something as simple as who controls the remote, and end in the divorce court. So eliminate the dangers. Have two televisions if possible, and respect for the other's preferences if not. See shopping as a one-man or one-woman operation wherever possible – love has died more than once keeping vigil outside a changing room. You may be the better driver, but don't rub it in. If your partner sees the telephone as an extension of their arm, so what? There are worse crimes.

In a good relationship, each partner has respect for the other as an individual. That means they have no desire to mould the other into a carbon copy of themselves. So he votes Labour and you Tory? So what. She's a night-owl, you need your sleep – well, some nights she goes your way; then you grit your teeth and your eyelids and return the favour occasionally. Tolerance is the lubricant of good relationships.

Trial separation

If things aren't going well, a trial separation can be a good way to get some breathing space without throwing the whole relationship away too hastily. It gives you both time to think about things, decide what's important and what's not. You can choose whether to stay absolutely apart, or to meet occasionally as friends, rather as you did in the beginning. You can also see how it feels to be on your own again, but that won't help if you sit at home moping all the time. You need to get out and meet people before you can decide whether or not the miss of him or her is too much to bear.

It helps to set a date ahead to meet up and talk about things. Keep it business-like, and don't let it deteriorate into a recital of who did what to whom. The point is to think about the future, and how you can make things work if that's what you both want. Meet on neutral ground rather than somewhere where you were once happy. Nostalgia can cloud your judgement. Discuss what you both want from the relationship, and how the time apart has made you feel. If you both decide you'd like to make another go of things, accept that the old relationship is gone and you're starting again. If you've discussed where things went wrong, you can make new ground rules to prevent it happening again. However much you've missed one another, don't just dive back in as

T

though nothing was ever wrong. It your partner's messy habits drove you mad before, they'll do so again unless he or she changes their behaviour. But don't despise compromise. Your accepting his or her need to watch soccer in return for him or her letting you keep newts is a fair trade.

Trust

What do you do when you find that the partner you trusted has betrayed you? Perhaps it was simply an online affair, and the excuse is, 'I was only pretending; it didn't mean a thing.'

Perhaps it was a foolish mini-affair at the office, or a one-night stand. Or it may have been a full-blown affair that lasted for years. Whatever the betrayal, 'I'll never do it again,' is the mantra. Even if you believe them, it's hard to just put it behind you and move on. In the beginning of a relationship, each partner wants to believe they know everything about the other. In fact, most people leave a great deal of the past unrevealed. They may have strayed before they met you, but you prefer to believe they are squeaky-clean. That's why the discovery of a fall from grace is so hard to accept. Left untreated, a wound like that can fester and destroy any chance of rebuilding the happiness you once had. So the first thing to do, if you want to re-establish trust, is to acknowledge the hurt and all the circumstances that surrounded it. I don't mean an endless stream of questions –.was it better with him/her? Did you tell him about me? How could you do this to me? – I mean a sensible discussion of what happened, what might have led up to it, and how the pain can be alleviated. And a third party who is sympathetic but not involved can do much to help this process (*see* Help section).

The first thing to accept is that, whatever the betrayal, you are the one he or she wants to be with. Whatever they did, it was secondary to their desire to be with you – if not, they would be long gone. By confessing all, they hope to banish the guilt they feel. If you continue to raise the matter, to constantly bring the ghost of the past into the space you share, you are the one perpetuating the intrusion into your relationship by keeping it alive. If you can't accept that what happened is history – painful, but history nevertheless – then perhaps you need to consider ending the relationship. Relate can help here (see Help section).

Or is it you who has to confess you've sinned? If what happened really was a one-off, I think it's a pity to reveal it at all (*see also* Confession). It may ease your conscience, but it will put your partner through hell. A confession can be a sign of faith in the partnership, a desire to be totally open and preserve the relationship, at all costs. Some people can accept that, and move

T

on. Some can't. 'How can I ever trust again?' they say. So before you confess, ask who you are doing it for: is it to ease your own conscience, or to make things better for him or her. And if it's purely for yourself, don't do it. An uneasy conscience is the price you have to pay for having erred.

Two-timing

We grow up believing that when you give your heart, it's completely and for ever. That's what the songs say, anyway. The truth is that the majority of people can, and do, love more than once in a lifetime. But falling in love after bereavement or divorce is a lot easier to manage than feeling that you love two people at the same time. Talk to someone who is juggling two relationships, and you'll usually find they feel certain that both loves are equal; they are positive that neither can be given up; but they also feel ashamed of what they're doing. If one of their loves is someone they live with, that always worries me. For this reason: inevitably, living with someone means that life slows down a little. You have to keep a home going, you see them at the kitchen sink, or weary after a long day. You see their crumpled morning face, hear the occasional fart, and sometimes smell them on their way to the shower. The other lover is a different proposition. By the time you come face to face with them, they are usually groomed to the nth degree, eyes alight with anticipation of wicked whispers in darkened corners, and even more wicked sex, heightened by the fact that it probably has to be hurried, and is illicit anyway. You see my point? Put the lover into the domestic situation, and he or she could be just as humdrum as the one you already have.

Usually, two-timing is selfish and ultimately destructive, especially if one of your lovers is in your work space or, even more dangerous, within the family. The number of people, both married and single, who claim to be unable to choose between two lovers seems to be on the increase, and these are not sixteen-year-olds, they're mature men and women who are well aware that they're hurting both themselves and the people they love. They are playing with fire, because infidelity inevitably spills over into the wider family.

It can be hard to know where friendship ends and falling in love begins, but the sensible thing is to flee as soon as you suspect things are getting dangerous. And this particularly applies to internet infidelity. You think it's safe because you're not actually *doing* anything, but it is not. If your partner finds out, there will be pain; and the lover you think is contained within the computer could also turn up on your doorstep (see Social Networking).

T

Exes can be another danger area. If you've shared a lot, it's very easy, even after much acrimony, to imagine that you're still in love with your ex. If he or she still harbours feelings for you, this can lead to trouble. Studies conducted at New York's Stony Brook University suggest that, in an affair, stress hormones distort our perceptions, and we can mistake the physical cues of fear and excitement for the sensations of falling in love.

So what should you do if it happens to you? First, consider the possibility that you love neither partner, in which case make a proper ending. If, on consideration, you realise that the new entrant into your life is the love of your life and can't be done without, you have to withdraw from your relationship. If, on the other hand, you decide the first relationship is the one that still matters, don't just sink back into it. Love needs to be worked at, and communication must be strengthened so that the relationship becomes impregnable in the future. And that means no checking of the second person's Facebook account, no web-stalking, no quizzing his or her friends in the hope that you'll hear that he or she is pining. Unless you want to be back in a situation where every moment you fear detection, the cut has to be final and clean.

HE SAYS: Look back at history. All the great friendships were between men: Saul and Jonathan, Damon and Pythias, Butch and Sundance. . . can you see two women holding hands to jump off a cliff?

> *SHE SAYS: Before he moved in, he agreed to share the housework. And he keeps his promise – a clean 50-50 split: he makes the messes, you clear them up.*

HE SAYS: Personally, I think adultery is a form of paranoia. Why else would a man risk home and children and his mother-in-law's tongue?

> *SHE SAYS; The body has limits but the bra has none (God bless Lycra).*

HE SAYS: If you get a promotion, it's favouritism. If she gets one, it's equal opportunity.

> *SHE SAYS: Part of the trouble is that the sexes mature at different rates. A girl of seventeen is a woman. A youth of seventeen has knuckles that trail the floor, rampant acne, and spends his time arm-wrestling his best mate.*

HE SAYS: *Don't say 'Anything' when she asks you what you want for supper. In the first flush of romance, you say it, and she goes off to produce culinary gems. Once out of the honeymoon period, say, 'Anything,' and she may well accuse you of putting all the decisions on to her. If you tell her precisely what you want, she'll probably burst into tears because she's got in everything but the thing you chose. She's failed you, which is all your fault, she misses her mother, and she wishes she were dead.*

> SHE SAYS: *Before you erupt, be sure it's worth the aftershock.*

HE SAYS: *If you can get out of it, never go shopping with her. Take a simple thing like mayonnaise: does she want it with tarragon or mustard seed, the one with Paul Newman's picture on it, or the own-brand cheapo? The time she takes pondering in the salad aisle, you could have made the bloody thing from scratch. Shopping is a delusional state. Watch a woman trying to cram a size seven foot into a size six shoe in a sale, and you'll know what I mean.*

> SHE SAYS: *Men are relatively straightforward: supping, shagging and sport (not necessarily in that order).*

U

Unrequited love (aka crushes)

How often have I read those words: 'I love him so much, why doesn't he love me?' Or 'She'll never find anyone who'll worship her like I do.'

'I love him/her, so he/she should love me back,' is a statement that does not compute. If it did, we'd all shack up with the first person we fancied, and miss all the fun of shopping around. That's easy to say, but the fact is that seeing what you want and being told it's not for you is painful. To that common complaint, 'I love him or her so much: how can they not love me back?' the answer is, 'Why should they?'

The sad fact is that loving someone with all your heart guarantees you nothing. They don't feel the overwhelming emotion you feel. That's not their fault, nor is it yours. You haven't failed, it's simply that X factor, that curious thing that binds two people together, just isn't there, and it can't be

U

manufactured. It's tempting to imagine a world in which love would evoke love, but it seldom works that way, and when it does it's in a novel. That is no one's fault. The other person may appreciate your devotion, even like you very much as a human being, but they can't summon up sexual or emotional attraction simply because you feel it for them. Don't feel defeated, and don't for one moment imagine you'll never find someone who will love you as you deserve. Even if you'd managed to make that relationship, he or she would never have given you a 100 per cent. You need someone who will give back as much as they receive. Believe me, that is worth waiting for.

Before you give your heart, try to make sure there is a pair of hands at least interested in catching it. If it's too late for caution, don't think you will never recover from the pain. Hearts are durable things, given time. Lick your wounds, and try not to apportion blame. Of course he or she was foolish not to see your worth, but folly is not a crime. Harbouring a grievance against the one who didn't love you is not only unfair, it's a waste of time.

Be grateful that you have escaped from a relationship in which you would have done all the loving – and perhaps received less than you deserve in return.

U

HE SAYS: You don't know women till you move in together. Everybody snores, so why single you out? You don't give her the elbow every time she snores — and sometimes she can sound like a steam engine going up Snowdon. When you lived with your mother, you only needed to say, 'I'd love a coffee,' and it was there, hot and fragrant. Now you say, 'I'd love a coffee,' and she says, 'So would I. Two sweeteners.'

> *SHE SAYS: Two wrongs don't make a right, but they make a good excuse.*

HE SAYS: You're watching a grudge match, Everton v. Liverpool. Does she snuggle up in time-out or a commercial (which would be OK)? No. She waits until the centre-forward's taking a penalty and then she wants a snog. Right at that moment! When you fend her off (as gently as possible), she takes the hump and changes the telly to the Discovery Channel.

> *SHE SAYS: Man's achievements are indeed impressive, but do they take account of man's freedom to concentrate on the task in hand while woman multi-tasks: holding down jobs, rearing children, running homes, coping with ageing relatives (his and hers), and reminding him he's due at the dentist?*

Unrequited love

HE SAYS: What man on the brink of meaningful sex has ever said to himself, 'I'll pay for this'?
But pay you will.

> *SHE SAYS: Adulterers are like politicians: they think they can fool all of the people all of the time.*

HE SAYS: With some women, it gets physical. They jab you with a pointed finger whose tensile strength equals that of tungsten. You, being a man, cannot retaliate. She, being a woman, trades on this.

> *SHE SAYS: You think you've found Mr Right, and find he's Mr Never Wrong*

HE SAYS: If there's ever World War III, the toilet seat will have started it. If they want you to put it down when you're finished, surely they should put it up when they're done? And the fuss over missing the bowl! Is it so difficult to deal with what is, after all, only modified H_2O?

Vices

A good relationship can weather most storms, but where a vice – a bad habit that takes over life – is concerned, professional help is needed. Gambling, alcohol, sex, smoking, addiction to pornography ... whichever it is, don't imagine it will cure itself. If alcohol is the problem, remember that all alcohol is empty calories, almost as many as pure fat. Choose small glasses rather than the buckets they tend to hand out nowadays. And if you start to see a drink as necessary to unwind, acknowledge that you have a problem. Women should not drink more than two to three units a day, and a standard 175ml glass of wine is two units, a large 250 glass three. A pint of standard lager is 2.3 units, and strong cider contains 4.7 units a pint.

Gambling can be fun, once in a while and well within the limits of your pocket. If you find you *need* to gamble, even mildly, seek help, especially if you're going into debt to play.

V

Smoking kills – or, at least, dismantles your health. If you want a future, never mind a relationship, give up smoking and enlist your lover's help to do so. If he or she is the smoker, you need to show them the undisputed facts of nicotine addiction. That should be enough, but if it's not, don't give up. Whatever the vice, working as a partnership you can make an improvement – in rare cases, effect a cure. But the best advice I can give is to reach out to the experts in whatever is your particular problem, and do it as soon as possible (see Help section).

Victims

You've had several disastrous relationships, and now you're convinced you're jinxed. No matter what you do or say, history will repeat itself, you think, and you'll be dumped again. Or perhaps you've dated a series of commitment-phobes, or heavy drinkers, or bullies. 'It's me,' you say. 'I attract them.' Is there any truth in that? Well, maybe a smidgen.

If you become accustomed to a pattern you can begin to accept it as the norm, and even subconsciously seek it out. So, the first disaster is a shock and completely accidental, but when the next one comes you're almost expecting it. This, you think, is what happens to you; you must deserve it, it's your fate. We know that's poppycock, but when you're hurt

V

and demoralised it's very easy to believe it. Perhaps you had childhood experiences that have skewed your thinking. Your dad was a philanderer, therefore all men are, and when your first boyfriend betrays you it's the norm. Or your mother was a shrew, so when your girlfriend screams at you, well, that's how it is, isn't it? No point in fighting back. Once you start thinking like that you have become a victim.

Getting out of victim mode is not as difficult as it might seem. You first have to accept that you were not responsible for what happened, however many times it was repeated. Life was to blame, and probably your only crime was in not getting out the minute things started going wrong. You were slow to react because you had been brainwashed into thinking that was how it always is.

You have to re-programme yourself not to expect trouble, and to react quite forcefully if you meet it. You need to believe that, although you may encounter frogs or witches along the way, you are entitled to a prince or princess, and you'll put up with nothing less. Turn to the Help section for support in breaking free.

V

Virgins

It may surprise you, but it's not uncommon for both men and women still to be virgins in their late twenties or early thirties. And, equally surprisingly, they're often ashamed of it – although what is shameful about being selective beats me. When they do meet someone and want to begin a sexual relationship, they're tempted to lie and pretend to be more sexually experienced than they are. In my opinion this would be a mistake. Not only would there be practical difficulties in covering up your virginal state, but you'd be beginning a relationship with a lie, which is not a good idea.

Experts differ on the way to handle this. Some advocate staying shtum and trying to bluff your way through like a practised lover. Others suggest you tell your soon-to-be lover the truth in the hope that he or she will be both delighted to hear how choosy you've been, and anxious to live up to the honour of being your first lover by making it a gentle and wonderful experience.

If you're a man or woman faced with someone who has waited a long time for the right moment to begin their sexual life, my guess is that you'll feel flattered but also a little daunted by the responsibility. However, with your greater experience you can gently guide them until nature takes its course, and it becomes something they not only feel they can do but something they want

V

to do very much. If you feel ready to lose your virginity, my advice is to make sure you have read a good book or books on sex, and feel reasonably clued up about the subject. If you've been so wary of rushing into things, I imagine this will not be a first date, and therefore you have probably got to know one another well before sex was even contemplated. To me, that suggests that you will have come close enough to be truthful with one another. If you still have doubts, remember that Relate's sexual therapists will be happy to advise (see Help section).

HE SAYS: Highwaymen wanted your money or your life. Women want both.

> *SHE SAYS: You must never let the enemy know you're wounded. It only feeds his ego, and it is big enough.*

HE SAYS: Scientific studies have shown that men exposed to the female tongue over a prolonged period suffer damage to the cilia, or tiny hairs, in the cochlea or inner ear. Which is why most hearing aids appear on elderly men.

> *SHE SAYS: Be wary of any man who buys you Turkish Delight in bulk, especially if he tells you it's Turkish name is Rabat Lokum (pronounced 'Lakooom'). Make your excuses and leave, because he has a vision of you lying on a silk couch stuffing your face with Rabat Lokum while waiting for his sultan to devour you. You are a goose being stuffed for foie gras, and it's not a pleasant feeling.*

HE SAYS: At your mum and dad's silver wedding, the best man told how your dad pinched your mum's bottom in the typing pool and three months later they were engaged. If you pinched a bum in here, you wouldn't be out of intensive care in three months, never mind engaged.

What men want in a woman

Men's attitude to women is ambivalent. When they meet them, the thought most often uppermost in their mind is, 'When will she have sex with me?' At the same time they want to think they have found that rare thing, a woman who has kept herself pure especially for them. From then on they will be in a constant state of flux, struggling with lust versus the desire to say, 'I won a prize.'

Of course all men aren't like that. Some are as careful with their own sexuality as they like their women to be. And although young men may like to have a scantily clad blonde on their arm to impress, the more mature man wants a woman he can be quietly proud of. Someone, in fact, whom he sees as the mother of his children. And if he's had to put a fair amount of effort into securing his prize, all the better.

He also wants a woman who has a life, not someone

W

whose only ambition is to circle around him like a planet circling the sun. It helps if his friends approve of her, and if that approval is mutual. He's prepared to forgive past mistakes, but not if they're flaunted. He wants her to be independent and spirited, but appreciates the odd moment when she plays the little woman needing a big, strong man. And if the chemistry is right and she really is the woman for him, all the above becomes meaningless (see X Factor).

What women want in a man

Nowadays women's first thought is not, 'Could he support me?' She is quite capable of supporting herself. But she is looking for strength in a man, the kind of strength that makes her feel emotionally secure. She wants him to want her, but needs to feel that sex is meaningful. And although she wants to know he desires her, if he tries to get into her bed two minutes after they've met it's a definite turn-off.

Almost from the beginning she will want someone who shares her vision of the future, even though she may not yet see the two of them having a common future. She wants someone she can be proud to show off, not in a foolish Hollywood way but because he is courteous and helpful to strangers. Above all, she wants someone who wants her, whose eyes are on her not straying towards the blonde across the room. But, as with men, when there is X Factor all the above is toast (see X Factor).

When

The 64,000-dollar question is surely, 'When is the time right to have sex in a new relationship?' There cannot be a rigid rule, because sex between any two people is unique. There is a general consensus, however, that sex on a first date is not a good idea.

In his book *The Men Files,* Humfrey Hunter admits that, on meeting a woman, man has sex on his mind; but he also advises, 'If you like a guy, don't jump into bed with him too quickly.' In Hunter's opinion, the sooner you sleep with a guy, the greater the chance that nothing significant will follow. Of course, there are cases where two strangers meet and are seized with such passion that sex is inevitable. In most cases, however, it's best to save the passion for later on, to be enjoyed at leisure.

W

Who wears the pants?

The phrase 'I'll have to ask the wife,' belongs to a bygone age, and research suggests that if a man's social life is run by his partner there's trouble ahead. The University of Chicago contends that men need their male friends, masculine pursuits, the chance to discuss things with friends without reference to 'Her Indoors'. Without this contact, sociologists believe a man can experience a loss of self-esteem that can even lead to sexual problems: a man whose wife is a constant presence when he meets his friends is 98 per cent more likely to experience erectile dysfunction. In other words, men have a need of other men as friends, and time apart from partners where 'boys can be boys' (*see also* Organisation, and Friends).

Workplace

Someone once estimated that a quarter of relationships were made in the workplace. I don't know whether this is true, but it's certainly true that many lasting partnerships did start in that way. However, if the workplace is somewhere where romance can strike, it is also the place where it can cause havoc, so here are a few guidelines:

W

- Working closely together on a project can create the illusion of romance, so be sure of your feelings.

- If you get a crush on a colleague, don't pursue it in working time. Don't pursue it at all, unless you have reason to think your attentions are welcome.

- Most workplaces have their scalp-hunters, male and female. Make sure you're not their next victim.

- Don't confide in colleagues until you are certain that your feelings are returned, and only then by mutual agreement.

- Never, ever discuss your intimate relationship with others in the workplace. It puts them in an embarrassing position, and it could spell doom for the romance.

- If the affair ends, remember that you are being paid to work, not to wreak vengeance on someone you think treated you badly.

- Don't immediately put in for transfer, or ask him/her to do so. You may get back together. If not, if you're old enough to get into a relationship, you're old enough to get out of it with grace.

W

Worth it

No matter how sensational the sex, however good the good times, there may come a time when rows or episodes of uncaring, even mere thoughtlessness, make you ask yourself, 'Is it worth it?' It goes round and round in your head. 'If I stay, I'll be hurt again. If I go, I'll be lonely.' 'He can change.' 'She doesn't mean it.' It's at times of indecision like this that you need to think clearly. It helps to see things written down. How many times in the last month were you truly happy? How many times were you near to tears?

If promises to change were made, how long was it before those promises were broken? If your thoughts are too jumbled to look back clearly, then keep a diary for a while, and see your life unfold on paper. If the bad days, the dark moments, outweigh the good, you need to act. Perhaps something can be done.

What's certain is that things won't change unless one, or preferably both, of you takes action. Relate or Marriage Care will help with any relationship problem (see Help section).

The wrong type

There's no doubt that some people are attracted to the wrong type. By 'wrong' I mean someone who is unlikely to bring them happiness, and almost certain to bring them grief. When you find yourself with the wrong type once you can call it bad luck. When it happens for the fourth time, acknowledge that you are subconsciously seeking trouble. Sometimes this can be a result of bad things happening in childhood, or youth. Subconsciously, you are seeking the dominating parent, the happy-go-lucky first love, the carbon copy of someone charismatic who occupied your growing up.

The bad thing about multiple relationships with a wrong man or woman is that they convince you that you are either jinxed or at fault in some way. In other words, to blame for it all. That can make you retreat altogether from seeking love. And it's crazy. Counselling can help you reset your senses, so that you know when it is time to quit and move away from someone who, however desirable now, will mean trouble later. Or help you, hopefully, avoid them in the first place (*see also* Victims).

HE SAYS: Women know how to conduct a row. First comes the silent treatment. They can hear you all right – the captain of a trawler off the Dogger Bank can hear you – they just choose not to. Serious requests, such as, 'Where's the first-aid box? I've ruptured an artery,' will be met with, 'Don't ask me'. Sometimes they'll recite a monologue to some mythical person. 'He wants to know where the first-aid box is? Let him find out. Why should I care? Did he care when I almost fractured my ulna three years gone Easter? Did he, hell!'

The one thing you must never do is say, 'Speak to me, please – not the wall.' This is to risk physical assault. The wisest move is to start whistling Peter and the Wolf while making a cat's cradle with some string. It throws them.

Your average woman could repel a cruise missile if she put her mind to it. Look at history: who burned people at the stake? Not Charles I or II; it was Elizabeth and Mary. Then you've got Boudicca and Amazons, and how do we know Attila the Hun was male? Attila sounds like a feminine name to me. I bet they ran the Inquisition. That's where they mastered the art of the pitiless question. 'What are you really thinking?' Half the time you're not thinking anything, you're just sitting there with a blank mind. I call that harmless. Your average woman calls it 'deliberate'. That's how unreasonable they are.

Give them a ring and say you'll be late, and you get the third degree. That's how they make you lie. It's not that you don't want to tell them you're having a swift half with the lads, it's that they wouldn't believe you if you did tell them. I mean, we're made out to be the bad ones, but look a bit closer . . . it's women behind everything. They can even see through walls.

X-factor

You can lay down rules about relationships, enter people for computer-matching, make sure they have everything in common, and the same goals in life . . . and have it end in tears. For a successful relationship, there has to be that mysterious ingredient, X Factor. If X Factor is there, the most unlikely coupling can succeed. No one who claims to understand human nature can deny its existence. What is it? Some say it's pheromones: you can't see or smell them, but they draw you irresistibly to the other person. I've spent years trying to pin it down, and I can't. I only know that for a relationship to be entirely successful it needs to be there. And it can often occur in people whom, at a glance, you would never fancy. Sometimes it strikes like lightning, sometimes it's a slow burn, so don't assume on first meeting that it isn't there. If you find it in someone and they find it in you, grab one another and don't let go.

SHE SAYS: The one thing men seem to miss is that women need to feel valued before they can give and receive good sex. Women need to be wooed.

> *HE SAYS: She's picking on you: you're too loud, too silent, too lazy, too interfering. In other words, you can't win. And then she says the fatal words: 'Mum thinks . . .' Well, frankly, it's not up to her mother to think anything. It's her daughter you're shagging, not her – and, yes, that's coarse, but it's also true.*

SHE SAYS: It constantly amazes me that people will put up with such crummy relationships. You'd take back an orange if, on peeling, it turned out to be a lemon. When a great romance begins to resemble the St Valentine's Day Massacre, do lovers turn and flee? Do they, heck! They stay on, inflicting or enduring wounds, while mouthing phrases like, 'He's lovely when he's sober.'

> *SHE SAYS: It constantly amazes me that people will put up with such crummy relationships. You'd take back an orange if, on peeling, it turned out to be a lemon. When a great romance begins to resemble the St Valentine's Day Massacre, do lovers turn and flee? Do they, heck! They stay on, inflicting or enduring wounds, while mouthing phrases like, 'He's lovely when he's sober.'*

Yearning

We all experience it at times, that almost unbearable longing for some thing, some place, some person. Well used, it energises you into striking out for what you want. Hopefully, the yearning ends when you achieve fulfilment. If it doesn't, then you have to be very careful not to allow yearning to turn into hopeless longing that blinds you to anything else in life. The saddest words in the English language are 'if only', so if your yearning has gone on for a long time without any sign of fulfilment, *move on*.

SHE SAYS: Happy co-existence requires that you ignore some facts.

> *HE SAYS: You do your bit. Put stuff in the laundry basket, throw the duvet back to air, leave her some hanging space in the wardrobe. So why the need for 'His Jobs' and 'Her Jobs' on the board in the kitchen? What more does she want? She has you in her bed — that should count for something.*

SHE SAYS: Diamonds are said to be a girl's best friend. Dogs are man's. I ask you, which sex is smarter?

HE SAYS: That's why women can't understand the rules of sport: whole areas of their brain are given over to remembering second cousin Lily's anniversary and sending the appropriate card.

> *SHE SAYS: On one side is his mother, who wants her darling boy all to herself but if he wants you, so be it. On the other side is your family, who understandably don't want to lose you. A bidding war breaks out. His mother offers to buy a sofa. When your mother hears that, she offers to buy two sofas. Three months later they no longer speak, and you have to use ropes to swing from room to room, so closely packed is the furniture and assorted bric-à-brac.*

Zest

Sometimes relationships just go flat. No one's fault; they've simply run out of steam. Before you call it quits, why not try injecting a bit of zest into things? What is zest? It's joy of life. It's being a bit mad for once; it's making love in a new way; it's blueing a bit of the wedding savings on one smashing night out; it's going the extra mile to find just the right birthday gift; it's saying 'I love you,' without its having to be extracted from you with tweezers; it's that look across a crowded room that says, 'You're the best thing in here.' It may work. If it doesn't, you'll certainly have improved your life experience.

Z

In the Zone

There's an awful period after break-up when, however much you want to move on, you feel a zombie. You know the feeling. You're over the guy/gal, you've cleared out their gear, deleted them from your phone and Facebook, and broken the news to your mum. You've done everything by the book, but you're still in the Zone. You almost fear going out into life again; you can't be bother to dress up because no one who matters will see; even preparing food can seem beyond you, so you nibble on whatever comes to hand and wash it down with something that does nothing whatsoever for your mood.

In the beginning, I wouldn't fight the Zone. You need a breathing space during which your brain and your body can adjust and begin to realise the possibilities that exist out there. Make an announcement to anxious friends and family that on a certain date, say two weeks hence, you will re-emerge, whole. Spend the first week chilling out (except when at work) by doing nothing. Play sentimental music, and have a good cry if you want to; watch telly wall-to-wall; or read; or go running, as long as it's aimless and not to a target. The second week should be planning, booking appointments for whatever treatment or excursion you feel you need, sorting your wardrobe, or buying in if you need to. There's a new life waiting which could, just possibly, be a lot better than the old one.

Z

It's possible that your Zone will be different. You won't feel bereft because you haven't let go. You always texted him or her at midnight, unless you were together, so at midnight you pick up your phone. OK, you're not pleading for reconciliation – not directly. You're simply asking if he or she is all right, and have they remembered their mum's birthday? Absolutely harmless, you think. You were together a long time, so it's only good manners. Except that it's really a subconscious attempt to put back the clock. And if you're not careful you will find good reasons to go on making contact day after day after day. As long as you do that, you'll stay in the Zone, tied to a relationship that has withered, whether or not you like it. There's a whole wide world out there which may contain something good. Get out there, and find out.

Help and advice

ACAS
www.acas.org.uk
Tel 08457 47 47 47
Helpline for free and impartial advice about employment rights, rules and disputes

Adults affected by adoption (NORCAP)
www.norcap.co.uk
Tel 01865 875000
Provides a range of specialist services for adults affected by adoption

The Beaumont Trust
www.gender.org.uk
Tel 07000 287878
Offers support help and information to those affected about Transsexualism and Transvestism and by the issues they raise.

Adviceguide
www.adviceguide.org.uk
08444 77 20 20 (Wales)
08444 111 444 (England)
Adviceguide is a public information website produced by Citizens Advice Bureau (CAB)

Association of British Introduction Agencies (ABIA).
www.abia.org.uk
Tel 020 8742 0386
Dating agencies and introduction agencies throughout the UK

Beat (beating eating disorders)
www.b-eat.co.uk (beating eating disorders)
Tel 0845 634 1414 Helpline (over 18)
Tel 0845 634 7650 Youthline (up to 18)
Help on all aspects of eating disorders including Anorexia Nervosa, Bulimia Nervosa, Binge Eating Disorders.

British Association for Counselling and Psychotherapy
www.bacp.co.uk
Tel 01455 883300
A professional body representing counselling and psychotherapy in the UK

British Association for Sex and Relationships Therapy (BASRT)
www.basrt.org.uk
Tel 020 8543 2707
Provides an information service, and help finding a therapist in any area

BPAS (British Pregnancy Advisory Service)
www.bpas.org
08457 30 40 30
Provides help to women with an unplanned pregnancy, or a pregnancy they choose not to continue with

Brook Advisory Centres
www.brook.org.uk
Tel 0808 802 1234
Advise for under 25s on contraception, harmful situations, terminations, STIs etc

CALM (Campaign Against Living Miserably)
www.thecaimzone.net
Tel.0800 58 58 58
Helpline for men aged 15 – 35 years

Care for the Family
www.careforthefamily.org.uk
Tel 029 2081 0800
Support to help individuals and families though good and bad times

CCCS (Consumer Credit Counselling Service)
www.cccs.co.uk
Tel 0800 138 1111
Free telephone and on-line help and advice re Debt

Citizens Advice Bureau (CAB)
www.citizensadvice.org.uk
www.adviceguide.org.uk
Tel 08444 111 44 (UK)
    08444 77 20 20 (Wales)
Advice on rights concerning cohabitation, divorce, finance, legal rights, property etc .

Community Service Volunteers (CVS)
www.cvs.org.uk
Tel 020 7278 6601
Information on all types of voluntary work

Counselling Directory
www.counselling-directory.org.uk
0844 8030 240
Website with information about different types of counselling and psychotherapy. Search for a counsellor or psychotherapist near you

Cruse Bereavement Care
www.crusebereavementcare.org.uk
0844 477 9400
Offers free, confidential help to bereaved people

Depression Alliance
www.depressionalliance.org
Tel 0845 123 2320
Provides information packs on depression

Divorce Care
www.divorcecare.com
Support groups to help in understanding divorce and its effects

Divorce Recovery Workshops
www.drw.org.uk
Tel 07000 781 889
Workshops of six, two hour sessions run at various locations in the UK

Do-it - Volunteering made easy
www.do-it.org.uk
On-line search for local volunteering opportunities

Family Lives (previously Parentline plus)
www.familylives.org.uk
Tel 0808 800 2222
Free 24 hour helpline for anyone in a parenting role.

Families need Fathers
www.fnf.org.uk
Tel 0300 0300 363
Concerned with problems of maintaining a child's relationship with both parents during and after family breakdown

FPA
www.fpa.org.uk
Tel 0845 122 8690
Information, advice and support on contraception, sexually transmitted infections, pregnancy choices, abortion and planning a pregnancy

Institute of Family Therapy
www.ift.org.uk
Tel 020 7391 9150
Providers of family therapy and psychotherapy
Volunteering England

Gingerbread
www.gingerbread.org.uk
Tel 0800 018 4318
Provides free advice and practical support for single parents

Home Start
www.home-start.org.uk
Tel 0116 258 7900
Provides help, support, friendship and practical assistance for families with children

Infertility Network UK
www.infertilitynetworkuk.com
Tel 0800 008 7464
Supports those trying to conceive with information or advice for their fertility or infertility

International Coach Federation (ICF)
www.coachfederation.org.uk
A resource for those seeking a coach

London Lesbian & Gay Switchboard
www.llgs.org.uk
Tel 0300 330 0630
Provides information, support and referral services for lesbians, gay men, bisexual, trans people and anyone who needs to consider issues around their sexuality.

Marriage Care
www.marriagecare.org.uk
Tel 0845 660 6000
Whether single, living together or r married provides support and counselling for relationships difficulties

MIND
www.mind.org.uk
0300 123 3393
Information and help for people with a mental health problem via a telephone helpline and 180 local Mind associations.

Miscarriage Association
www.miscarriageassociation.org.uk
Tel 01924 200 799
For those affected by miscarriage, ectopic pregnancy or molar pregnancy – information and support to help you through.

Money Advice Service
www.moneyadviceservice.org.uk
0300 500 5000
Advice to help you make the most of your money.

NAPAC (The National Association for People Abused in Childhood)
www.napac.org.uk
Tel 0800 085 3330
Telephone support, counselling and information for people abused in childhood plus relationship difficulties

National Council for the Divorced and separated
www.ncds.org.uk
Tel 07041 478 120
Information, support and social events for the divorced and separated

National Council for One-Parent Families
see Gingerbread

National Debtline
www.nationaldebtline.co.uk
Tel 0808 808 4000
Helpline providing free confidential and independent advice on how to deal with debt problems

National Family Mediation
www.nfm.org.uk
Tel 01392 271610
Network of Family Mediation Services countrywide that offers help to those affected by family breakdown, separation and divorce

The National Federation of Plus Areas of Great Britain
www.18plus.org.uk
Social events for people aged 18 – 35

NHS Direct
www.nhsdirect.nhs.uk
0845 4647
Health advice 24 hours a day 365 days a year

One Up
www.oneupmagazine.co.uk
Tel 01787 223557
Online magazine for single parents and step parents

Parentline Plus
See Family Lives

Relate
www.relate.org.uk
Tel 0300 100 1234
Offers Relationship Counselling, Family Counselling, Children & Young People's Counselling, Sex Therapy and Courses and Workshops.

The Samaritans
www.samaritans.org
Tel 08457 90 90 90
Confidential emotional support 24 hours a day

SANE
www.sane.org.uk
Tel 0845 767 8000
Provides care and emotional support for people with mental health problems, their families and carers

Shelter
www.shelter.org.uk
Tel 0808 800 4444
Free housing and homelessness advice and information

SOLO
www.federation-solo-clubs.co.uk
Many clubs affiliated to the National Federation of Solo Clubs which provide a regular venue at which to meet and to take part in various managed activities

SurvivorsUK
www.survivorsuk.org
Tel 0845 122 1201
Help, support for men (over 18) who have experienced childhood sexual abuse or adult sexual assault / rape, as well as their partners and carers

The Tavistock Centre for Couple Relationships
www.tccr.org.uk
Tel 020 7380 1960
Provides specialised couple counselling and psychotherapy

THT - Terrence Higgins Trust
www.tht.org.uk
0808 802 1221
Offer a range of services to suit the varied needs of our diverse communities - about all aspects of HIV

The Way Foundation (Widowed And Young)
www.wayfoundation.org.uk
Tel 0300 012 4929
WAY aims to support young widowed men and women as they adjust to life after the death of their partner – whether that was a month, a year, or ten years ago.

Women's health concern
www.womens-health-concern.org
Tel: 01628 488065
Advice line and email service with specialist nurses to help educate and support women with their healthcare

Young Minds
www.youngminds.org.uk
Tel 0808 802 5544

Addictions

Adfam (Families Drugs and Alcohol)
www.adfam.org.uk
020 7403 0888
For people worried about someone else's drinking

Alcoholics Anonymous
www.alcoholics-anonymous.org.uk
0845 769 7555
Information and help with alcoholism and problem drinking

Alcohol Concern
www.alcoholconcern.org.uk
Tel 020 7264 0510
Services for people whose lives are affected by alcohol-related problems

Al-Anon Family Groups UK
www.al-anonuk.org.uk
Al-Anon 020 7403 0888
Alateen 020 7407 0215
Provide support to anyone whose life is, or has been, affected by someone else's drinking

Battle Against Tranquillisers (BAT)
www.bataid.org
0844 826 9317
Help and support for people addicted to tranquillisers or sleeping pills

Council for information on tranquilisers and anti-depressants
www.citawithdrawal.org.uk
Tel 0151 932 0102

Gives support and information for individuals, families, friends and professional advisors dealing with prescribed tranquillisers, sleeping tablets, and antidepressants

Drinkline
www.drinkaware.co.uk
0800 917 8282
Telephone advice and referrals to other sources of help

Drugscope
www.drugscope.org.uk
Tel 020 7520 7550
Informative website; DrugScope is the national membership organisation for the drug sector

Frank (National Drugs Helpline)
www.talktofrank.com
Tel 0800 77 66 00
Helps you find out anything you need to know about drugs.

Gam-Anon
www.gamanon.org.uk
Tel 08700 50 88 80
If you are affected by someone else's gambling; Gam-Anon can help

Gamblers Anonymous
www.gamblersanonymous.org.uk
Website with a search for local meetings. No need to phone or make an appointment. Just turn up

Help Porn Addiction
www.helpaddictions.org
Website with information and sources of help with the problem of porn addiction,

Domestic Violence

Mankind
www.mankind.org.uk
Tel 01823 334 244
Supports male victims of domestic abuse

Men's Advice Line
www.mensadviceline.org.uk
Tel 0808 801 0327
Advice for men experiencing domestic violence

NAPAC (The National Association for People Abused in Childhood)
www.napac.org.uk
Tel 0800 085 3330
Telephone support, counselling and information for people abused in childhood plus relationship difficulties

NSPCC (National Society for the Prevention of Cruelty to Children)
www.nspcc.org.uk
Tel 0808 800 5000
Child protection helpline. Runs a range of services for both children and adults, including helplines
and local projects

Rape and Sexual Abuse Counselling Service (RASAC)
www.rasac.org.uk
Tel 01962 848018
Confidential listening and support service for women and men who have been raped

Refuge
www.refuge.org.uk
0808 2000 247
Freephone 24 hour national domestic Violence helpline run in partnership between Women's Aid
Supports women and children who experience domestic violence and can provide accommodation

Women's Aid
www.womensaid.org.uk
0808 2000 247
Freephone 24 hour national domestic Violence helpline run in partnership with Rufuge
Supports a network of over 500 domestic and sexual violence services across the UK

Legal

Citizens Advice Bureau (CAB)
www.adviceguide.org.uk
Tel 08444 111 44 (UK)
     08444 77 20 20 (Wales)
Advice on rights concerning cohabitation, divorce, finance, legal rights, property etc.

The Divorce Bureau
www.thedivorcebureau.co.uk
Tel 0800 730 9831
Matches people with a local solicitor experienced in matrimonial issues

Law Centres Federation
www.lawcentres.org.uk
Tel 0845 345 4 345
Law Centres are not-for-profit legal practices providing free legal advice and representation to disadvantaged people

Rights of Women
www.rightsofwomen.org.uk
020 7251 6577
Legal advise line: domestic violence and abuse, relationship breakdown including issues relating to children

Index

Main page references are in **bold**

A
Abortion *see* termination
Abuse *see* domestic violence; harassment
Adultery *see* affairs
Advertisements *see* classified ads
affairs **7–10**, 114–16, 149–50
    attitudes to 7, 114
    and boredom 27–9
    reasons for **7–9**, 23–4, 27–9
    serial adultery 187–8
    surviving 114–16
    two-timing 218–20
age differences 10–11
alcohol **227**, 257–8
anger
    and confrontation 45–6
    on ending relationships 28
anti-depressants 66–7
aphrodisiacs 11
apologies 183–4

appearance
    and attraction 11–15
    and dating 64–5
    see also erotic capital
arguments 16–19, 45–6
    causes 16–18
    over driving and cars 73–4
    resolving 18–19, 45–6
arrogance 77
attitudes
    to infidelity 7, 114
    to sex before marriage 7
attraction 191, 203
    and appearance 11–15
    in men 191
    sexual 41
    signs of 196–7
    and status 38–9
    in women 203

B
Background *see* upbringing
baggage **21–2**, 184

bereavement 22–3, **138**, 251, 256
betrayal 8, 22, **23–4**
    signs of 78–9
    see also affairs; infidelity; trust
biological clock **25–6**, 112
blame 30–1
blind dates 57
blushing 162
body dysmorphic disorder 14
body language 26–7
boredom 27–9
Botox injections 13
breaking up **29–33**, 177
    licking your wounds 133–5
    putting it off 171
    reactions to **30–2**, 48–9, **208**, **246–7**
    signs of **195–6**, 238
breast surgery 13–14
buying love 33, 99

C

cars 73–4
casual sex 192–3
celibacy 190
charisma 35
chat-up lines 40, **198–9**
chemistry *see* X-factor
child bearing
    and age difference 10–11
    and fertility 25–6
children 36–8
    importance of having 43
    partner's 22, 36
    your own 36–8
class divide 38–9
classified ads **63–4**, 84
clothes 14–15
commitment **40–1**, 54–6, 176–7
    see also engagement
communication *see* talking
compatibility **41–4**, 194–5
compliments 44
confession 217
    effect on partner 45
confidence 12
confrontation 45–6
contraception **47**, 249
controlling 47–8
    see also domestic violence
cosmetic surgery 13–14
cosmetics 15
crushes 223–4

D

dance classes 51–4
dating 57–66
    agencies 63
    blind dates 57
    first dates **64–6**, 126, 235
    a friend's ex 93–4
    internet dating **57–60**, 143
    paying for 147–8
    singles events 60
    singles' holidays 62–3

speed-dating 60–2
death of a partner **22–3**, 251
decision making
    after a break up 30, 32
    and doubts 70–1
    and independence 112–13
dependence 113
depression **66–7**, 251, 253
desperation 125
dieting 12–13
differences 177
    in relationships 41–4, 194–5
dignity 68, 125, 178
discussion *see* talking
domestic violence **69–70**, 259–61
doubts 70–1
dream lover 71
    see also expectations
drifting apart 72–3
    see also boredom; breaking up
driving and arguments 73–4
drug addiction 118
dumped 30, 68, 74
    see also breaking up; victims

E

eating disorders **13**, 249
ego 77
    see also self esteem
emails 77–9
embarrassment 162
emotional intelligence 79–80
emotional maturity 11
engagement 80–1
erotic capital 81–2
exes
    sexual history 193–4
    your own **82–3**, 219
    your partners 82–3
expectations 84
    see also dating; holidays

F

Facebook 99, 100, 125, **200–2**
fairy tales 87
    see also dream lover; expectations
faking orgasm 87
family
    attitudes to new partners 39
    confiding in 30, 32, 71
    importance of 43
    in-laws 116–17
fantasies 88–9
    living out 8
father figures 89
faux pas 161–2
fear
    of being alone 29–33
    of a partner 48–9, 69–70
fertility 10–11, **25–6**, 252
fidelity 7–10, 149–50
first dates **64–6**, 126, 235
first love 154
flirting 89–90

forgiveness 23–4, **90**
fraudsters 179–80
friends 235–6
    attitudes to new partners 39
    with benefits 192–3
    confiding in 30, 32, 71, 125
    dating a friend's ex 93–4
    keeping 91–3
    partner's 92

G
gambling **227–8**, 257–8
game-playing 97–8
    see also gold-diggers; love rats; scalp-hunters
getting back together **98–9**, 126
gifts 33, 99
giving 100 per cent 100–1
gold-diggers 101
great loves 115
grieving 22–3, **138**, 251, 256
grooming 15
growing apart
    see boredom; breaking up; drifting apart
guilt 101–2
    and children 37
    living with 45
    over failed relationships 8, 31
    signs of 78
guilty secrets **102–3**, 216–17

H
habits **105**, 227–8
hang-ups **106**, 168–9
harassment 106–7
holidays 107
    holiday romances 108
    for singles 62–3
honesty 102–3

I
identity 111, 159
    see also independence
impotence 190–1
in-laws 116–17
independence **112–13**, 235–6
infidelity 7–10, **114–16**, 149–50
    attitudes to 7, 114
    and boredom 27–9
    reasons for **7–9**, 23–4, 27–9
    serial adultery 187–8
    surviving 114–16
    two-timing 218–20
insecurity *see* hang-ups; pornography
insomnia 67
instinct 27
internet
    dating **57–60**, 143
    infidelity 219
    pornography 167
issues 118

J
jealousy 121–2

K
keen (too keen) 125

L
laughter 129
letters **129–30**, 133
libido 131–2, 189
licking your wounds **133–5**, 166
lies **135**, 143, 193–4, 201
listening **135–6**, 211
living together 150–1
loneliness 29–33, **136–7**
long distance relationships 137–8
loss 22–3, 138
love 139
    unrequited 223–4
    see also X-factor
love rats 101, 179–80, 202

M
make-up 15
making contact 141
making up 126
marriage 8–9, 42–4
maturity, emotional 11
meeting new people 142–3
    dance classes 51–4
    dart board analogy 54–6
    see also dating

memories 23
    see also nostalgia
men
    attitudes to women 233–4
    attractive qualities 191
    as breadwinners 41, 205
    and commitment 41, 205
    confidence 12
    coping after divorce 31
    expressing emotions 162
    fertility 10–11, **26**
    need for friends 235–6
    sex drive 26
mischief 144–5, 201
mobile phones 145–7
money **147–9**, 250, 254
monogamy 149–50
mood 150
mother figures 89
mourning **22–3**, 251, 256
moving in 150–1
moving on **133–5**, 166, 175, 243, 246–7
mutual respect 112–13, 204–5, 214

N
neediness 83, 112
    see also self esteem
negativity 153
newspaper ads *see* classified ads
no for an answer 153–4
non-surgical intervention 13–14

nostalgia **154**, 215

O
occasions 157–8
organisation 158–9, 235–6
orgasm 160
    faking 87

P
partners
    control freaks 47–8
    crazy 48–9, 69–70
    exes **82–3**, 219
    previous children 22, 36
    running down 181
    sexual history 193–4
    taking for granted 9
past *see* exes; upbringing
personality *see* identity
pets, custody of 33
pheromones 241
photographs 165–6
pity 166
pornography **167–70**, 257–8
pregnancy **212–13**, 249
    see also contraception; fertility
pressure 170–1

Q
que sera sera 173

R
rebound 175
reconciliation 24
relationships 176–7
    after bereavement 22–3
    and boredom 27–9
    escaping from 8
    getting back together **98–9**, 126
    long distance 137–8
    moving on **133–5**, 166, 175, 246–7
    and mutual respect 112–13, 204–5, 214
    new 42–4, 184
    reasons to end 24, 27–9
    second time around 184
    stages of 54–6
    working at 100–1, 117
    see also breaking up
religion 177
remorse 101
reparation 102
resentment 16, 19
responsibilities
    and arguments 18
    sharing 41
revenge 177, **178**
romance 150, **178–9**
    giving up on 28
romance fraud 179–80
    see also internet

rows *see* arguments; confrontation

S

scalp-hunters 101
second time around 184
self esteem 122, 183, **184–6**
    and body image 13, 14
    and domestic violence 69
    neediness 83
    see also ego
sensuality 187
separation 137–8
    reasons for 24
    trial 214–15
serial adultery 187–8
sex 188–96
    casual 192–3
    drive 26, 131–2, 189
    faking orgasm 87
    and fantasies 88–9
    frequency 189
    insecurity about 194
    before marriage 7
    refusing 155
    safe 195–6
    sexual attraction 41
    sexual compatibility 194–5
    sexual history 193–4
    sexually transmitted diseases 195–6
    therapy 191, 249
    when to start 56, 64, **235**
    without strings 192–3
shock after a break up 31
shopping 214
singles events 60
sleep 197–8
small talk 65, **198–9**
smoking 223–4
snooping 77–8, 145–6, 200–2
social
    social class **38–9**, 205
    social gaffs 161–2
    social networking 200–2
socialising 137, 143
sorry, saying 183–4
soul mates 84
    see also dating
space 203
speed-dating 60–2
spinning 204
stalkers *see* harassment
standards, shared 42–4, **204–5**
status 38–9, 205
stonewalling 206
stress 170–1
    and arguments 18, 19
    and sex 189
sulking 206–7
support organisations 31
surgical intervention 13–14
survival 30, **208–9**

T

talking 211–12

about money 147–9
best time for 18
with children 37–8
importance of 100–1, 137
to sort out arguments
    18–19, 46
teenagers, maturity of 11
termination 47, **212–13**, 249
texting 145–7
tit for tat affairs 10
tolerance 42, **213–14**
toy boys 10
trauma 21–2
    childhood 188
trial separation 214–15
truce objects 19
trust 137–8, **216–17**
    see also betrayal; lies;
snooping
two-timing 218–20

U
understanding 79–80
unfaithfulness *see* betrayal;
infidelity
unrequited love 223–4
upbringing **21–2**, 116, 188,
229, 239, 253

V
vaginismus 190
vices 227–8, 257–8
victims **228–9**, 239

violence *see* domestic violence
virgins 230–1

W
weight 12–13
widowhood *see* bereavement
women
    attitudes to men 234–5
    attractive qualities 203
    confidence 12
    coping after divorce 31
    dieting 12–13
    dissatisfaction with
appearance 14
    fertility 10–11, **25–6**
    loss of libido 131–2
wooing *see* romance
workplace 236–7
    affairs 115
worth it 238
wrong type 239
    see also victims

X
X-factor 39, 223, **241**

Y
yearning 243

Z
zest 245

If you've enjoyed this book, and would like to find out more about Denise and her writing, why not join the Denise Robertson Book Club. Members will receive special offers, early notification of new titles, information on author events and lots more. Membership is free and there is no commitment to buy.

To join, simply send your name and address to info@deniserobertsonbooks.co.uk or post your details to The Denise Robertson Book Club, PO Box 58514, Barnes, London SW13 4AE

Novels by Denise Robertson include:

The Stars Burn On • Endgame
Act of Oblivion • The Winds of War
The Tides of Peace • A Relative Freedom
The Promise • None to Make You Cry
The Second Wife • The Bad Sister
Wait for the Day • The Beloved People
Strength for the Morning • Towards Jerusalem

All Denise's novels are available from good book shops price £7.99
Alternatively you can order direct from the publisher by calling the credit card hotline 01903 828503 and quoting DR10TP1

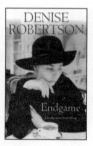
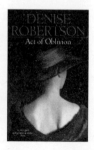
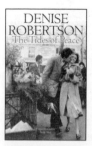
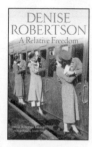
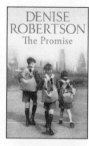

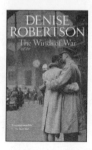
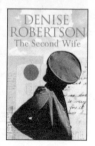
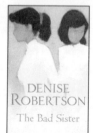
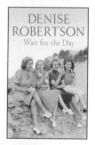
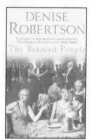

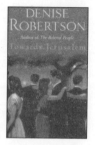